CHRISTIAN RACE REALISM

Published by Sacra Press.

Michael Spangler, *Christian Race Realism*.
Edited & designed by Cody Justice.
© 2025 by Sacra Press

Sacra Press
www.sacrapress.com
contact@sacrapress.com or sacrapress@gmail.com

First edition.
Printed in the United States of America.

Go to www.sacrapress.com for more Reformed, right-wing, & classic
books, to become a sponsor of future works, and to enjoy alternative
Christian music of Psalms & Saints.

Godspeed and goodwar.

CHRISTIAN RACE REALISM

by
Michael Spangler

SACRA PRESS
SACRA AD GLORIAM DEI

CONTENTS

Dedicatory Epistle to President Donald J. Trump

TO THE PRESIDENT OF THE UNITED STATES, the Honorable Donald John Trump, your humble servant Michael Spangler wishes all health, blessing, and peace in JESUS CHRIST, the King of kings and Lord of lords.

Inasmuch as your election to the office of our chief executive was a sign of our great people's expectation that you would serve their best interests, especially in defending them from enemies, we dedicate this work to you in hope that it may give you help in powerfully protecting us in our great need.

For our need is truly great. Indeed to our beloved nation the prophet could speak as he did to Israel of old, "Your country is desolate, your cities are burned with fire: your land, strangers devour it in your presence, and it is desolate, as overthrown by strangers" (Isaiah 1:7). The godly in our land do mourn with desolate Jerusalem, "Our inheritance is turned to strangers, our houses to aliens. We are orphans and fatherless, our mothers are as widows" (Lamentations 5:2). And we cry out to God, and under God, to you his servant, given the sword to punish evil doers, "Rid me, and deliver me from the hand of strange children, whose mouth speaketh vanity, and their right hand is a right hand of falsehood" (Psalm 144:11). We join our voice with God himself as he addresses "the congregation of the mighty," judging "among the gods," that is, the princes of the earth who are like God in that they rule, among which gods you now yourself presently hold preeminent position, "Defend the poor and fatherless: do justice to the afflicted and needy. Deliver the poor and needy: rid them out of the hand of the wicked" (Psalm 82:3–4).

We write, I say, with humble expectation that this book may help you in these matters, as you are a minister of God to us for good (Romans 13:4). Our present crisis calls for many goods to be administered to us, but among them we would name the two goods which this present work is chiefly crafted to promote and to defend. The first good is that of our nation's racial heritage. "We the people of the United States of America," those whom our presidents affectionately call, "My fellow Americans," have an identity, and that identity does not entirely subsist in land, in law, in customs, or in language. Behind those characteristic marks stands a real flesh-and-blood people, the same people that conquered the savage wilderness of our vast continent, that wrote our laws and carefully passed down our customs, that spoke our mother tongue which we received from England, that framed our Constitution to "secure the Blessings of Liberty to ourselves and our Posterity." This same people from the beginning of our life under the noble Union of our States identified its own distinct and real ethnicity, as "one united people, a people descended from the same ancestors," in the words of Jay. In their first law concerning immigration, they built a high wall to keep out all those who would dilute their distinct racial heritage, requiring in 1790 that all who would be naturalized must be, like them, free white persons of good character. They further protected themselves by law from harmful marriages with other races, and by tariffs and other sensible trade laws—which we rejoice to hear that you have promised to restore—carefully kept the riches of our land as the possession of the race who had with blood and toil conquered and cultivated it.

We White Americans exist today as such because of our forefathers' zeal to preserve our national family and its unique inheritance. Their provident care for their posterity is why our country still today is filled with millions of familiar faces, white and ruddy, and goodly to look to, and why our people still enjoy evident prosperity and privileges. Indeed, despite the flood of darker foreigners who have most recently invaded us, we Whites are the majority, and we still rule, in business, academics, law, science, medicine, and politics. The reins of American power have been firmly held by White men's hands for our entire history. This is true even of the office you now hold. The one recent exception, by your own confession, cast an exceedingly dark shadow over our beloved land.

Moreover, we would humbly attest that it was by the suffrage of our race, your fellow White Americans, and in particular, White evangelicals, that your election to our highest office was decided. "We the people," the very "posterity" considered in the Constitution, listened with bated breath to your inaugural address, and cheered your declaration of a "golden age" in which America would reclaim her native greatness. Yet, if with meekness we may note our disappointment, you gave explicit thanks to "African Americans, Hispanic Americans, Asian Americans," and "to the Black and Hispanic communities," but none to us. Was there no credit left to spare for your own people? The very race that built our country, that spilled its blood in all her wars, that though most hated and maligned today, devotes its sweat and tears and treasure for the country's good, even the good of foreign guests? No word of recognition for the race that chose you for our President, against hope hoping that through your kindness we might find "a little reviving in our bondage" (Ezra 9:8)?

We ask again, not to exceed our place under your rule, but only to make a humble plea, as children to their father, Why now in both your presidential terms have you made such show of special privileges for Jews? We see your zeal to combat "anti-Semitism," and we beg you, where are the orders to combat widespread "anti-Japhetism" (that is, hatred of Whites, the sons of Japheth, Genesis 9:27), and in particular, "anti-Americanism," which those same Jews, and many others with them, publicize with full impunity? In this we say again, we need your help. We need your presidential power to be applied, as our founding fathers explicitly intended, for the defense, support, encouragement, and blessing of their own posterity. Please, Mr. President, hear our concerns. Dismiss them not because of their unpopularity. Help White Americans. According to your promise, make us great again.

If we may continue in our humble boldness, the second good that we have need to ask from you, a good that in itself, and in God's sight, excels the first as far as heaven excels earth, is the civil direction of our nation to its chief and highest end, that end which children of Presbyterians, such as yourself and your own mother, have repeated now for centuries: "To glorify God and to enjoy him forever."

This glorification and enjoyment God commands of men and nations, promising to bless them for it, "Blessed is the nation whose God is the LORD" (Psalm 33:12), and threatening a curse for failing in it, "For the nation and kingdom that will not serve thee shall perish; yea, those nations shall be utterly wasted" (Isaiah 60:12). Moreover, he established it as the chief end of civil rulers, that as ministers of God (Romans 13:4) they would serve the Lord with fear, and kiss his Son, lest he be angry and they perish from the way (Psalm 2:11–12). This duty you must do, and it being given directly from the Lord, it is more solemn and important than any promise to uphold a human constitution, or desire to please an earthly people. Indeed, the oath you swore at your inauguration was made before this glorious God, and therefore contained by implication an oath of all the duties that you owe him, as his creature, and his servant in the civil sphere.

This duty to honor God calls you, and our whole nation with you, to certain particulars. First, personal confession, of your sins, and of the true religion, and that with true sincerity. Without a living faith in Jesus Christ, without repentance, without holiness, no man of any rank will see the Lord (John 14:6; Luke 13:3; Hebrews 12:14). Nor can the highest earthly king rule fittingly without submission to the King of kings (Revelation 19:16). The noble kings of Judah—David, Solomon, Josiah, Hezekiah—showed that civil dignity and personal piety most sweetly comply, and so they ought in rulers of every time and place.

Second is national repentance, that like the king of great Assyria in Nineveh at Jonah's preaching, you would by both example and decree call us to put on sackcloth, fast, and sit in ashes, crying mightily to God, declaring to the people, "Let them turn every one from his evil way, and from the violence that is in their hands. Who can tell if God will turn and repent, and turn away from his fierce anger, that we perish not?" (Jonah 3:8–9). How fitting this response would be to the great judgments now upon us, as God has given us over to the power of cruel foreigners (Deuteronomy 28:43–44), and of our own perverted lusts (Romans 1:26–32). And how fitting such humility would be to your oft-expressed desire to make America great again, for as Christ said, "He that shall humble himself shall be exalted" (Matthew 23:12).

Third, and not to be neglected, is a ruler's duty, as a father to his people, to see their spiritual needs be met, and their spiritual harm prevented. This requires that all public blasphemy should be suppressed, our laws restored that helped our people keep the Christian Sabbath, our churches purged from heresy and wickedness, and given civil help in their spiritual task to preach the Word, and win our people's souls again for Christ. In this we would see fulfilled the promise given by Isaiah to the believing church, "And kings shall by thy nursing fathers, and their queens thy nursing mothers" (49:23), "Thou shalt suck the breast of kings: and thou shalt know that I the LORD am thy Savior" (60:16).

We must be sober here: God has a quarrel with our nation. Its federal indifference toward religion has seeped down into the States, and to their people, such that a spiritual lukewarmness, carelessness, and even outright godlessness has taken hold, from which only the deepest humiliation and repentance can rescue us. Yet difficult as it may be, such repentance remains the duty of our nation, and of our President to lead us in it. We fervently implore our God that he would give the grace to see this duty done, despite the cost.

This wielding of the power of your sword, your purse, your influence to promote religion in our land, is in God's providence inseparable from the first duty we pled for, the care for our White race. For White men, in God's kindness, are the heirs of Christendom. Moreover, the particular Northwestern European tribes that joined their blood to make our own, in their blessed Reformation enjoyed a heavenly favor far above all other peoples. Our Pilgrim fathers, zealous Protestants, settled our coasts "for the glory of God, and advancement of the Christian faith." We honor both our race, and true religion, by laboring to see their Compact kept in our own day. Our noble Christian fathers' blood runs in our veins. We ought to spend the strength conveyed by it unto the glory of their God.

Our plea in brief is, we would beg that true ethnic Americans be recognized and defended as the native possessors and the lawful heirs of our great country, and that this country and its people be directed by your power to seek the Lord with all humility and zeal. In simple terms, we want America for the Americans, and we want America for God and Christ.

In pleading all these things, I beg God also for all blessing, health, and strength upon you, your family, and our nation, and in all things remain your humble servant,

Michael Spangler
March 7, 2025

Chapter 1:
Introduction

Race is real.

In the recent past most everyone agreed with this. Even children knew that "red and yellow, black and white" described real differences among mankind. And yet today, especially among White Christians, it seems quite common to deny it. "One race, the human race" is heard in pulpits, in church magazines and academic journals, and on social media.

To quote but one example:

> Perhaps the most important thing to say about race, in the typical American sense of the word, is that it does not exist. Unlike sex, it has no biological reality, and unlike ethnicity, it has no cultural reality. The human community simply is not divided into half-a-dozen (or whatever) racial groups united by distinct genetic markers or a common culture.[1]

---

1   David Van Drunen, "Reflections on Race and Racism." Ordained Servant, March 2021: https://www.opc.org/os.html?article_id=874

This denial of race and its importance is a serious error, and a deadly one. Satan knows race is real, and is presently abusing its reality with great success. His servants on the left teach that "Whiteness" is very real, and very bad. They notice "White privilege" (their term of spite for God's real blessings on White men) and hate it, as the greatest evil on the earth. As Susan Sontag said, "The white race is the cancer of human history."[2] And the only solution to this White cancer is its utter eradication.

Another of their prophets said:

> The goal of abolishing the white race is on its face so desirable that some may find it hard to believe that it could incur any opposition other than from committed white supremacists.[3]

The distinction such men make between eliminating Whiteness and killing White people themselves is, as this quote shows, so thin as to be meaningless. They are gunning for White genocide. And so far it appears they have had good success: by feminism, birth control, abortion, demoralizing propaganda, war, pornography, perversion, and replacement through unfettered non-White immigration, the White man is, in relative terms, dying with alarming speed in his own

---

2   Susan Sontag, "What's Happening in America." John S Haplin, November 27, 2012:   https://johnshaplin.blogspot.com/2012/11/whats-happening-in-america-1966-by_8613.html

3   Noel Ignatiev, "Abolish the White Race," Harvard Magazine, September-October 2002:   https://www.harvardmagazine.com/2002/09/abolish-the-white-race-html   —   See   more   about   Ignatiev   here: https://www.aljazeera.com/opinions/2019/11/17/abolishing-whiteness-has-never-been-more-urgent

lands. Consider this graph showing the trend of demographics in America:

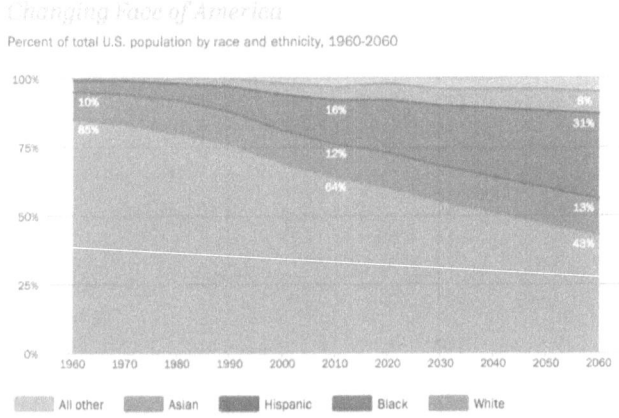

Nor is this merely a reduction in proportional demographics. Look at what happened to the livelihood of Whites in 2021:[4]

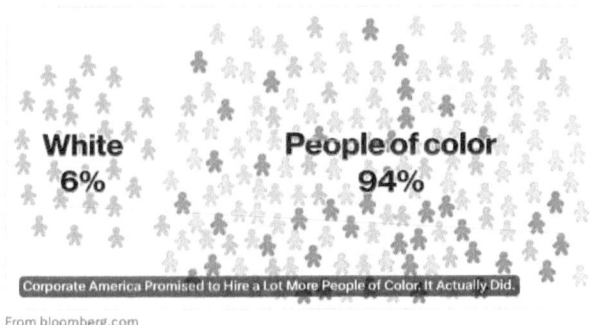

From bloomberg.com

4   "Corporate America Promised to Hire a Lot More People of Color. It Actually Did." Bloomberg, September 25, 2023: https://www.bloomberg.com/graphics/2023-black-lives-matter-equal-opportunity-corporate-diversity/

Nor is this merely an American phenomenon. Humza Yousaf, the former First Minister of Scotland (though himself a Pakistani), in 2020 gave a now-notorious rant against the predominance of White Scots in their own country. In South Africa, political rallies feature thousands shouting, "Kill the Boer!" This caught public attention last year:[5]

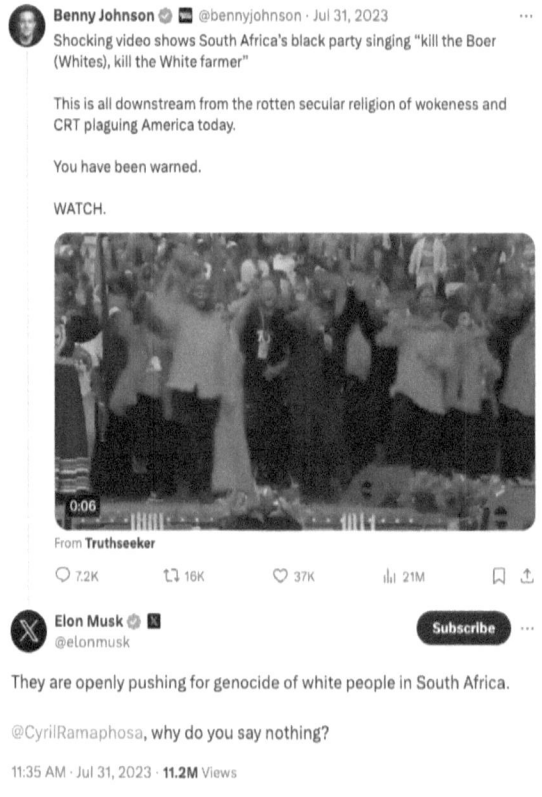

5   https://x.com/bennyjohnson/status/1686025436667518976?s=20
    — The New York Times assured us "it should not be taken literally"—
    https://www.nytimes.com/2023/08/02/world/africa/south-africa-
    kill-boer-song.html

A name often used to describe this war on the White man is the "Great Replacement." Sometimes its proponents try to fool others by denying its existence.[6] But often they just celebrate it openly.[7] Joseph Biden did so in this video,[8] in which he said:

> Folks like me who were Caucasian, of European descent for the first time in 2017 will be in an absolute minority in the United States of America, absolute minority. Fewer than fifty percent of the people in America from then and on will be white European stock. That's not a bad thing. That's a source of our strength.

For anyone that still suspects this claim of widespread global anti-White hatred is a baseless "conspiracy theory," the recently-published book by Jeremy Carl, *The Unprotected Class: How Anti-White Racism is Tearing America Apart*,[9] proves it is real, beyond all doubt.

This Satanic anti-White ideology they call "anti-racism," but it should be clear, it is not anti-race. They believe firmly that race is real, and that Whiteness, which is real, is evil.

White men, and especially White Christians, seem largely ignorant of this threat to their existence. But most of those who are actually aware of it propose a solution that makes matters worse. They think they have cut the Gordian Knot,

---

6 "The Racist 'Great Replacement' Conspiracy Theory Explained." SPL Center, May 17, 2022: https://www.splcenter.org/hatewatch/2022/05/17/racist-great-replacement-conspiracy-theory-explained

7 https://x.com/tomselliott/status/1526698619390382080?s=20

8 https://x.com/VivekGRamaswamy/status/1731888060848132097?s=20

9 Jeremy Carl, *The Unprotected Class: How Anti-White Racism Is Tearing America Apart*, Regnery Publishing, 2024.

when standing above it all they say, the problem with the "woke" is that they even care about race. "Colorblindness," as they call it, is their proposed solution: "One race, the human race."

But a moment's thought should show this does not solve, but only dismisses the problem. If race isn't real, then the White race isn't real, which then implies it doesn't matter that it's being destroyed. The "Great Replacement," if it exists, is not important. Race, they say, is only a social construct, so if one so-called race disappears, all that is lost is a mere theory, an academic fiction that enlightened people have no reason to uphold. "Good riddance to race" in our day necessarily means, "Good riddance to the White race." With such a "conservative" anti-race-realism, Satan and his anti-White servants are all too happy to agree.

Such senselessness on race could be merely laughed off the stage, if its proponents were not so deadly serious. Within the White church these ideas are treated as unquestionable. It is not only that White men with names and platforms teach it (recall Van Drunen above). White leaders also threaten and enact grave punishments on fellow Whites who disagree. The "racist," the "kinist," the "White nationalist," the "White supremacist"—all terms describing White race realists—are mercilessly hounded by church power. If you doubt this, read this Aquila Report article[10] (originally published by the leftist

---

10 Sonia Scherr, "Presbyterian Denomination Roots Out Racism." The Aquila Report, June 4, 2010: https://theaquilareport.com/presbyterian-denomination-roots-out-racism/

Southern Poverty Law Center)[11] on what happened to an elder in the Presbyterian Church in America.

Or see this post from an influential Baptist professor:[12]

Denny Burk ✓
@DennyBurk

Kinism is a theological heresy. Churches must confront it as they would any other false teaching—through admonition, discipline, and excommunication.

Titus 3:10-11, "Reject a factious man after a first and second warning, knowing that such a man is perverted and is sinning, being self-condemned."

2 Timothy 3:5, "...holding to a form of godliness, although they have denied its power; Avoid such men as these."

8:03 PM · 11/27/22 · Twitter Web App

Or another such bold condemnation from a Presbyterian:

Presbycast ✓
@presbycast

If you love the church please don't make racialists and kinists church officers. The New Testament gives no support to such fleshly ideologies and instincts. In fact, it opposes them.

9:46 PM · Sep 3, 2023 · **13.6K** Views

---

11 https://www.splcenter.org/fighting-hate/intelligence-report/2010/church-denomination-roots-out-racism
12 https://x.com/DennyBurk/status/1597033290979868672?s=20

For longer examples of such denunciation, see this article[13] by Doug Wilson, or this address[14] by Owen Strachan. It appears from all these things that anti-race-realism is the White church party line, which no one may cross with impunity.

But it gets worse. While some men push "colorblindness," others push leftist racialism. A particularly sad example is Dr. Ligon Duncan, a celebrated churchman, who wrote a foreword to Eric Mason's "anti-racist" book, *Woke Church*.[15] In it Duncan asks regarding his past lack of awareness as a White Christian of the so-called sin of racism,

> How could I have been so utterly blind to my context? How did a sin that had pervaded my whole world growing up not even register to me as something to help preachers address…?

And then he charges his forbears with gross twisting of Scripture:

> Specifically, during the eras of slavery, segregation, and civil rights, some of our best theological minds figured out how 'love you neighbor' did NOT apply to the racism and injustice (and, by the way, I mean injustice the way the Bible defines injustice) that black people were experiencing, oftentimes at the hands of professed Christians.

---

13 Douglas Wilson, "My 360° Whiteness Review." Blog & Mablog, November 14, 2022: https://dougwils.com/books-and-culture/s7-engaging-the-culture/my-360-whiteness-review-comes-in.html

14 Owen Strachan, "Christianity and Kinism." G3 Ministries, October 18, 2023: https://youtu.be/fK72GG-nWgk?si=RRk1HdIEOXSyrmij

15 Eric Mason, *Woke Church: An Urgent Call for Christians in America to Confront Racism and Injustice*, Moody Publishers, 2018.

Duncan concludes regarding the book's author, "I look forward to sitting at his feet to listen and learn."[16] This is not to mention Duncan's 2021 address[17] celebrating the replacement of Whites as "God's plan to reverse secularism in the United States."

Whether it's Eric Mason, or Jemar Tisby,[18] or Mika Edmonson,[19] or Ekemini Uwan, a Westminster Seminary graduate, who declared, "Whiteness is wicked,"[20] many are teaching the principles of leftist anti-racism, often with explicit support from White church leaders.

What do we make of this? Our own pastors preach race isn't real, punish their people for insisting otherwise, then praise those who teach leftist race consciousness, even as it fuels the fires burning down our nation and its churches.

This error and hypocrisy must be exposed, and against it the truth about race clearly taught and defended. To that end, this book will seek to demonstrate and deal with the reality of race. With the Lord's help, we aim in this chapter to define

---

16 You can read the whole forward in Google Books: https://books.google.com/books? id=B6dGDwAAQBAJ&lpg=PP1&pg=PT17#v=onepage&q&f=false

17 https://x.com/WokePreacherTV/status/1791443871211167866

18 https://www.facebook.com/story.php? story_fbid=3819480341506152&id=100003326704087

19 Staff Writer, "Woke TGC Contributor Suggests Mary Taught Jesus The Sermon On The Mount," Protestia, June, 2022: https://protestia.com/2022/06/17/woke-tgc-contributor-suggests-mary-taught-jesus-the-sermon-on-the-mount/

20 Jessilyn Lancaster, "Black Theologian Stirs Controversy After Telling Women's Conference 'Whiteness Is Wicked,'" Charisma News, April 11, 2019: https://charismanews.com/news/us/black-theologian-stirs-controversy-after-telling-women-s-conference-whiteness-is-wicked/

"race realism," and in particular "Christian race realism," and in the following chapters to prove, defend, and apply it.

I: Race Realism Defined

Race realism is the recognition that mankind is divided into distinct races, that the differences between the races are large and relatively permanent, and that this racial diversity ought to be acknowledged, celebrated, and defended.

Note the elements of this definition.

Mankind. We do affirm "one human race."

Distinct races. But we also affirm that the one race of man is divided into narrower races. In common English usage, "race" is flexible: it can speak of ethnicity on any scale, from all mankind, down to single tribe or clan. In this book we will most commonly use "race" to speak of the largest ethnic divisions of mankind.

These divisions are variously described. To mention a few options:

Sometimes we hear of two: White and non-White. More often of three: White, Black, and Brown. Or of four: Red or Amerindian, Yellow or Asian, Black or African, and White or European. Or of seven, as in the options given in the U.S. Census: White, Hispanic or Latino, Black or African American, Asian, American Indian or Alaska Native, Middle Eastern or North African, and Native Hawaiian or Pacific

Islander. We could also speak in terms of biblical and ancient history, of Semites, Hamites, and Japhethites.

This variety is not necessarily contradictory, nor does it mean that discerning racial boundaries is impossible. It reflects the fact that divisions can be made according to different criteria (e.g. appearance, region, historical origin), and with varying levels of specificity and rigor. But even if there are irreconcilable differences among such class-ifications, it is not more than exists when attempting to explain the order of reality in any other field. Compare biologists' debates over the taxonomy of non-human creatures: none take the fact of disagreement as a proof there are no meaningful distinctions to be made.

Moreover, we will sometimes distinguish "race" from "ethnicity" or "nationality," using the latter two to speak more narrowly, usually according to presently established boundaries between nation-states: e.g. among Whites, of English, Germans, or Dutch. If others use these terms differently, this is no real problem, as long as we agree in substance, that there are large ethnic categories that transcend family, clan, and nation, and that they are real.

The differences between the races are large. This means that race is not a matter of mere skin or mere geography (though we may name races after their skin-color or country for convenience). Rather, race goes deep, extending as we'll show to countless other realities, physical, cultural, intellectual, moral, and spiritual.

And relatively permanent. We leave open here the question of racial change in the long term, of how new races may form by ethnogenesis, of peripheral cases where the races overlap, and of exactly how all racial difference is passed on (nature v. nurture, genetics v. epigenetics, etc.) These questions are interesting and useful in their place, but exact determination of them lies beyond the scope of this series. Racial differences arise and persist predictably and permanently enough that for all practical purposes, race is immutable. Whites are white, and Blacks are black, and will remain so for our entire lifetime and beyond.

Racial diversity. We understand this term, not like the multiculturalists, as a ploy to colonize White nations with non-Whites, and make Whites ashamed of their own race and history, but as a grateful recognition of the fact that man exists in distinct races, and that in itself, this is a good thing.

Ought to be acknowledged, celebrated, and defended. Here we outline the application: we must name, praise, and protect racial distinctions. As in all other matters, we must think and live according to reality. The application will of course stir up the greatest opposition, but truth not practiced might as well not be taught. If race is real, real duties follow.

II: Christian Race Realism

This is the race realism we set out to defend. What, then, of our title, "Christian Race Realism"?

Christian race realism is no different in substance from what we've just defined. Truth itself is not changed when Christians affirm it. Christians ought to recognize that many non-Christians see racial realities, and many do so better than we do. In the fight for truth we ought to acknowledge our unbelieving allies, and even learn from them, even as we flee yoking ourselves together with their unbelief.

That said, we do seek and expect certain benefits from a self-consciously Christian presentation of these truths on race. First, by it we may supplement natural arguments, persuasive in their own right, with scriptural testimonies, which are divine, infallible, and unanswerable. We underline the word of creation with the word of the Creator himself: "Thus saith the Lord." As we will see in the next chapter, Scripture has much to say on race.

Second, by it we make more explicit the role of God's creation and providence in racial matters. God tells us that by creation he made man's race (Gen. 1:27), and that by providence he made man's races (Gen. 9–11; Deut. 32:8). As Paul says to the Greeks, God "hath made of one blood all nations of men for to dwell on all the face of the earth, and hath determined the times before appointed, and the bounds of their habitation" (Acts 17:26). This is a powerful antidote to materialist theories which employ race as a lever by which to pry men off from faith in God.

Third, by it we aim more directly and explicitly to apply these truths to the glory of God, which is man's chief end, and to the true good of man under God. This will preclude all godless and inhumane answers to hard racial questions.

Fourth, by it we pursue a more specific defense and application of these truths for Christian individuals, Christian families, Christian churches, and Christian nations. This is a necessary but thorny subject, and we cannot expect unbelievers to address it for us well.

Fifth, by articulating a sound Christian race realism, we would lay the foundation for future political application of these truths under a more Christian government, which according to God's promises, we long for and expect.

Sixth, we do this for the sake of our evangelism. Anyone with experience evangelizing in our egalitarian age knows, unbelievers often bring up questions about race. Moreover, if an unbeliever who is right about race realism hears the gospel from a Christian that he knows is wrong on it, it will be a barrier to his conversion.

III: Caveats

Finally, we would further clarify two matters so that we may not be misunderstood. First, race is natural, and earthly, and thus like all things under the sun, to set our heart on it is vanity and striving after wind. This does not mean race is not real, or not important. But race does not have ultimate importance. Heavenly things, God, Christ, the gospel, faith, hope, love, and so forth, are far more excellent. Grace excels race as far as heaven excels earth. Racial religious privileges are real, and can be a help unto salvation—God works in families, nations, and generations—but they never in themselves saved anyone. Paul, for example, speaks in this way of the privileges of Jews in Romans 9:1-8. There will be no ancestry test to enter glory: the sole criterion of the last judgment will be "faith which worketh by love" (Gal. 5:6).

Second, race realism is no excuse for error, sin, or schism. We have to underline this here, because of what we observed in the introduction, that even within the church, men will say the worst of those who would defend race realism, or the White race against its enemies. We assert here, and hope to prove beyond a doubt, that there is no inherent evil, falsehood, or scandal in the assertion of race realism. It is a truth of nature, and of Scripture—how could it then be blamed for sin?

Now, we would not join our enemies in exaggerating the sins of race realists. We would in fact plead with pastors and presbyteries, we race realists in your midst are not the godless troublemakers you have been told we are. If you would join the world in slandering us, you would be sinning, and also laying on us great temptation to respond in sin. This itself is a scandal, and schismatic.

Yet even so, we say here for all to see, that even under enormous pressure, race realists have no right to sin. We say this to clear our conscience, and our name. We testify that in this series our whole aim is to speak the truth in love, for edification, not destruction. May God bless our labors to that end.

Chapter 2:
Scripture

In the introduction we considered the need for the teaching of race realism in light of prevailing anti-White hatred and the church's failure to oppose it. We then defined race realism in this way:

Race realism is the recognition that mankind is divided into distinct races, that the differences between the races are large and relatively permanent, and that this racial diversity ought to be acknowledged, celebrated, and defended.

After explaining this definition, we gave our reasons in particular for pursuing Christian race realism. The first was our desire that, when considering this natural matter, we might hear not only nature, but nature's God, its Creator and Governor, as he speaks in his inspired and infallible Word, the Bible.

Now, as race is a natural matter, it would be appropriate, even natural, to begin first with natural arguments, such as we will present in the following chapter. Scripture itself presumes nature, and never contradicts it, even as it guides us to the right understanding of it. But we judged it best to begin first with the Bible, not only to honor the Holy Scriptures, but also to clear away doubts of our Christian readers, some of whom suspect that race realism is an ideology foreign to Christianity, with no warrant in the Word of God.

In considering what Scripture says on race, we will look first at God's creation and providence, then at Israel's civil law, then at some points from the New Testament.

I: Creation and Providence

And hath made of one blood all nations of men for to dwell on all the face of the earth, and hath determined the times before appointed, and the bounds of their habitation; that they should seek the Lord.[21]

This statement Paul made on Mars' Hill summarizes well what Scripture says on race, speaking first of creation, that God made one race of men, then of providence, that he ordered history in such a way that the one race became a multitude of separate nations.

So first, creation. God "hath made of one blood all nations of men." "God created man in his own image" (Gen. 1:27), and from the one man Adam, his wife Eve (Gen. 2:22); "Male and female created he them," (Gen. 1:27), from which two came the entire human race. Thus Adam called Eve "the mother of all living" (Gen. 3:20). There should be no doubt

---

21 Acts 17:26–27.

at all that Scripture says, man is one blood, one race, one large extended family.

Then second, providence. This is sometimes called by theologians "continued creation," as the same Creator who made the world in the beginning, by the same omnipotence upholds, directs, and brings to pass all things in that creation that have ever happened since. Paul says that God, by wise prior determination, made man "for to dwell on all the face of the earth," a fulfillment of his original blessing of man at creation, "Be fruitful, and multiply, and replenish the earth" (Gen. 1:28). Notice especially the manner in which God made man to fill the earth: "and hath determined the times before appointed, and the bounds of their habitation." That is to say, God's plan for man was not globalist egalitarian conformity, but nationalist particular diversity. He established each nation's peculiar time and place. That is to say, nations are real, and really distinct, by God's good providence.

Some would object here, Paul speaks of "nations," not of "races." But we should heed the apostle's warning "that they strive not about words to no profit" (2 Tim. 2:14). "Nation" in scriptural usage speaks of the same natural reality as our term "race." Both terms refer to natural divisions developed over time within the one extended family of mankind. The only difference is that compared to our usage of "race," "nation" in Scripture speaks of a narrower portion of mankind. But if the narrower and more specific is proven, why not the broader and more general? "Nation" in Paul's usage proves ethnic particularity is real, even more strongly than if he merely spoke of "race."

Moreover, it is not as if Scripture has no conception of ethnic categories broader than "nation" but narrower than "mankind." Genesis 9 tells of God's providential division of all men into three large races: "And the sons of Noah, that went forth of the ark, were Shem, and Ham, and Japheth.... These are the three sons of Noah: and of them was the whole earth overspread" (Gen. 9:18–19). Then Genesis 10 shows in detail how the more narrow nations or sub-races descended from these three. More could be explained here, but for our purposes it is enough to say, when Scripture speaks of the natural reality of nations, it by extension speaks of the natural reality of race. This is underlined in Genesis 10:32, "These are the families of the sons of Noah, after their generations, in their nations." Noah's three sons had widely extended "families" which we call "races," and these families developed over "generations" into "nations."

Let us now consider more specifically what the Bible says about the racial distinctions which the Lord has brought about by providence. It testifies to such distinctions in at least seven categories:

1. *Ancestry.* We saw this already in Genesis 9–10. The Bible does not speak scientifically of genetics, but it does tell us that man's "families" (races) and "nations" are produced by natural procreation, "after their generations" (Gen. 10:32). Race may be more than blood, but it is never less.

2. *Appearance.* The Bible recognizes that God in providence has made races look starkly different. It acknowledges some men are permanently black in skin, and uses it as an image of how all men are permanently black in heart: "Can the Ethiopian change his skin, or the leopard his spots? then may ye also do good, that are accustomed to do evil" (Jer. 13:23). The Hebrew there for "Ethiopian" is more literally "Cushite," but the parallel New Testament Greek term "Ethiopian" (Acts 8:27) means by etymology, "scorched face." Compare the likely etymology of the name "Ham" (father of Cush, Gen. 10:6), from a Hebrew root signifying heat or sun. The Bible lends weight to the ancient and modern speculation that Black men turned black because of generations of life under the hot African sun. Compare Song 1:5-6, "I am black, but comely.... Look not upon me, because I am black, because the sun hath looked upon me." Note moreover the change observed from white skin to black in Lamentations 4:7-8, "Her Nazarites were purer than snow, they were whiter than milk, they were more ruddy in body than rubies.... Their visage is blacker than a coal." It should be clear from these things, not only that Scripture recognizes racial color difference, but that it passes some aesthetic judgment on it. The Bible celebrates David as "ruddy" (a description proper only to fair skin), "and withal of a beautiful countenance" (1 Sam. 16:12; 17:42). It also praises Christ's purity and excellence under the image of white skin, "My beloved is white and ruddy, the chiefest among ten thousand" (Song 5:10).

3. *Geography.* We already saw regarding nations that God "hath determined...the bounds of their habitation" (Acts 17:26). Deuteronomy 32:8 confirms this, "When the most High divided to the nations their inheritance, when he separated the sons of Adam, he set the bounds of the people." As he gave to ancient Israel the promised land, so he apportioned to other nations their own places. Genesis 10:5 says specifically of Japheth's sons, "By these were the isles of the Gentiles divided in their lands; every one after his tongue, after their families, in their nations." Even the promises of salvation for nations outside Israel presume they live in different places. Gentile salvation thus is pictured as a pilgrimage: "And many people shall go and say, Come ye, and let us go up to the mountain of the LORD, to the house of the God of Jacob" (Isa. 2:3), "They shall ask the way to Zion with their faces thitherward, saying, Come, and let us join ourselves to the LORD" (Jer. 50:5).

4. *Language.* Scripture freely recognizes language as a marker of racial difference. Non-Israelites are "people of a strange speech and of an hard language, whose words thou canst not understand" (Ezek. 3:5–6), and even within Israel, the pronunciation of one Hebrew word, "Shibboleth," marked tribal boundaries (Judg. 12:6). Revelation uses "tongue" as a synonym of other more distinctly ethnic terms: "every kindred, and tongue, and people, and nation" (5:9; 7:9; 14:6). Consider also how Genesis 11 describes the origin of distinct languages. As man was just beginning to diversify into the separate races, still "the whole earth was of one

language, and of one speech," (v. 1). Linguistically-united man presumed at Babel to build a tower to reach heaven, and God punished his pretension with linguistic confusion: "Go to, let us go down, and there confound their language, that they may not understand one another's speech" (v. 7). The result of linguistic division was geographic division, and therefore racial division, by the course of isolated procreation over generations: "So the LORD scattered them abroad from thence upon the face of all the earth" (v. 8). Pentecost was not, as many assert, a reversal of Babel, at least insofar as it did not remove the natural diversity of language (or of race; note those speaking in tongues were Jews, and Galileans, Acts 2:1, 5–7), but only temporarily overcame it for spiritual ends, by an extraordinary work of the Holy Spirit. The division of man's races, as it was caused in part by the division of his languages, so it is proved by that division, which has only deepened since Babel. Moreover, it may be argued from Revelation 5:9 that diversity of tongues will remain in heaven, but whether or not this is so, though distinction of language did come in part as punishment, it is not sinful in itself, or any barrier in itself to spiritual unity among believers.

5. *Character.* Scripture also freely recognizes that, just as distinct nations reproduce, appear, are located, and speak distinctly, so also do they live and act distinctly. This is evident in their distinct national sins. In Isaiah 33:9, "a people of a deeper speech than thou canst perceive" are also called "a fierce people." So in Deuteronomy 28:50, "A nation

of fierce countenance." So also for Israel itself, which is distinguished in both Old and New Testament as "stiffnecked and uncircumcised in heart and ears," a people who "do always resist the Holy Ghost," as their fathers did (Acts 7:51; cf. Deut. 9:6; 1 Thess. 2:14–16). Remember the Canaanites, a race so grossly wicked beyond others that the just solution to their evil was annihilation (Deut. 7:1–4; cf. 9:5; Lev. 18:12). Compare Paul, who when speaking to the pastor of a church of Cretians, says of them without qualification, "One of themselves, even a prophet of their own, said, The Cretians are alway liars, evil beasts, slow bellies. This witness is true. Wherefore rebuke them sharply, that they may be sound in the faith" (Titus 1:12–13). Clearly in Christ there is hope that men of the most godless races may repent and "be sound in the faith." But just as clearly, men are not sound in the faith by nature. By nature, all men are dead in sins (Eph. 2:1; Rom. 3:23), and some races of men reveal that deadness in ways peculiar to their race.

6. *Power.* In recognizing such moral distinctions between nations, Scripture is decidedly not egalitarian: at least in some distinct respects, some nations are superior or inferior in virtue. This is also true regarding power. Over the course of history, some nations rule, others are ruled. Some are weak, others are strong. Though Israel was relatively small in number (Deut. 7:7), God made her "a great and mighty nation" (Gen. 18:18; cf. Deut. 4:7), and under Solomon, exceeding great, even over other nations (1 Kings 4:21). God also singles out certain heathen nations as particularly

mighty: for example, Daniel's prophecy describes the Roman empire as "strong as iron, forasmuch as iron breaketh in pieces and subdueth all things" (Dan. 2:40), and Luke gives us a glimpse of the fulfillment of that prophecy when Caesar Augustus decreed the taxation of "all the world" (Luke 2:1). It seems evident to us that this is also a fulfillment of the ancient promise to the grandfather of the European race: "God shall enlarge Japheth" (Gen. 9:27). Compare also in Genesis 9 the notable lack of blessing upon Ham, who shamed his father (v. 22), and the just curse of abject slavery pronounced upon Ham's son, "Cursed be Canaan; a servant of servants shall he be unto his brethren" (v. 25, again in vv. 26 and 27). Opinions differ on this passage, and agreement on its interpretation is not essential to maintaining race realism, but if later history sheds any light, it appears this curse on Ham's son Canaan is rightly taken also as a curse upon the father, and on his other children by extension. Whatever the case, "servant of servants" would aptly describe the future fate of many of Ham's Black African children.

7. *Religion.* Not surprisingly, according to its peculiar religious purpose, Scripture also identifies distinct races by their distinct religions. Consider the continual contrast of the LORD God of Israel over and against "all the gods of the nations" (Ps. 96:5) and "the idols of the heathen" (Ps. 135:15). Scripture recognizes the "gods of the Egyptians" (Jer. 43:13), and similarly the gods of Babylon (Isa. 21:9), and of the Sepharvaim (2 Kings 17:31; 18:34; cf. 19:12), though they are properly "no gods, but the work of men's

hands" (19:18; Gal. 4:8). And it also recognizes that such distinctive national idolatry is typically permanent: "Hath a nation changed their gods?" (Jer. 2:11). The Bible does hold out hope that the nations one day will abandon their false gods, but that will be a marvelous exception to the present state of things, only made possible by God's extraordinary grace (Ezek. 36:25), grace such as is evident in measure in the present ingathering of the nations under the New Testament (Matt. 28:19).

II: Israel's Civil Law

We have considered various testimonies to God's creation of man, and his providential distinguishing of mankind into races. Now we look specifically to the Mosaic civil law. This is not because we believe it must be copied and pasted intact into modern constitutions—it was a specific law for a specific people in specific circumstances, according to the nature of all civil law. However, it is still to be admired, studied, and imitated according to its general equity, that is, the universal natural and moral justice inherent in it. We are to look on ancient Israel's God-given civil law and say, "What nation is there so great, that hath statutes and judgments so righteous as all this law?" (Deut. 4:9). And at the least, we must assert that anything the holy God commanded for ancient Israel is in itself entirely free from sin. Therefore in principle it could never be immoral to enact similar laws in modern nations, if done with prudence according to their peculiar circumstances.

1. *Nationalism.* A profound Scriptural testimony to race realism is that Israel's divinely inspired civil polity is explicitly nationalist. Throughout it discriminates between native Hebrew Israelites, often identified in family terms as "the children of Israel," or "brethren," and others who were "strangers" or "sojourners" (see e.g. Deut. 4:44; Lev. 25:47; Deut. 1:16; 15:3; etc.). To put this another way, when their constitution spoke of the people for whom it was written, it spoke of them in terms of blood. By analogy with the Constitution of the United States, the Israelites could say their national founding document was written for "ourselves and our posterity." This does not mean assimilation of certain foreigners was never possible (as we will see below), but it does mean that *foreigners never defined the essence of the people.*

2. *Tribal land ownership.* One specific proof of the nationalist character of the civil law regarded land ownership. Israel, defined by blood, was also in some respect defined by soil, though less essentially (for the nation still existed when in exile). Moreover, the ownership of this soil was tied to specific bloodlines in a unique manner, God allotting not only large portions to each tribe, but also more narrow portions "by their families" (Josh. 13–17), which they were legally forbidden from transferring to other families or tribes, a restriction applied with careful prudence in the hard case of the daughters of Zelophehad (Num. 27; 36), and maintained

also by the requirement of restoration of purchased land in the forty-ninth year Jubilee to the families that originally held it (Lev. 25:8–10). Compare Naboth's noble resistance unto death when Ahab desired his vineyard, "The LORD forbid it me, that I should give the inheritance of my fathers unto thee" (1 Kings 21:3).

3. *Protectionist economics.* There were further measures in Israel's polity that righteously discriminated along racial lines. Nowhere in Scripture is slavery ever described as sinful; indeed, the holy God himself sanctioned it in his holy nation, but he did so with ethnic distinction. Foreigners could be enslaved for life, even in their generations (Lev. 25:44–46; cf. Josh. 9:23, 27; 1 Kings 9:20–21); however, "If thy brother, an Hebrew man, or an Hebrew woman, be sold unto thee, and serve thee six years; then in the seventh year thou shalt let him go free from thee" (Deut. 15:12), unless the Hebrew slave remained of his own will (Ex. 21:2–6). So also for charging interest on loans: it was lawful to charge "a foreigner," but unlawful to charge an Israelite "neighbor" or "brother" (Lev. 25:35-37).

4. *Rule by kinsmen.* So far we have seen that the polity God himself appointed recognized Israel as a distinct nation of men, defined by blood, and gave to that nation distinct privileges above ethnic foreigners. This becomes all the more clear when considering the legal requirements for leaders. The king had to be "one from among thy brethren," and "brethren" should not be spiritualized here to mean only a believer in the Lord: God specifies, "Thou mayest not set a

stranger over thee" (Deut. 17:15). In the first king, Saul, and in David's hereditary line that followed in the kings of Judah, this law was strictly kept, under strictly ethnic terms. Similarly, lesser magistrates were to be chosen from wise men "among your tribes" (Deut. 1:13–16), just as Jethro wisely counseled Moses after the Exodus to "provide out of all the people able men" (Ex. 18:21; cf. v. 25, "out of all Israel"). The equity of these requirements is evident: a people will be best ruled by their own men, who more than others will have a natural affection and interest in their peculiar good. Also evident is the inequity when strangers rule instead of kin. God counts it as a curse: "The stranger that is within thee shall get up above thee very high; and thou shalt come down very low" (Deut. 28:43; cf. v. 13; Isa. 1:7; Lam. 5:2).

5. *Segregation from foreigners.* The legal contrast between Israelite and stranger is also evident in the strict laws that segregated Israel from the surrounding foreigners. God built the "middle wall of partition" between Jew and Gentile (Eph. 2:14) to be high and strong. Though properly the dietary laws were ceremonial and religious, they had serious civil consequences: Jews could barely even eat with strangers, as much of their food was declared unclean (Lev. 11; cf. Neh. 13:3; Acts 10:14, 28). In specific as regards the Canaanites, they were not only to be avoided, but utterly destroyed (Deut. 20:17). God is very specific about the Canaanite nations in Deuteronomy 7:1–5: no covenant with them, no mercy unto them, no marriages with them (cf. Neh. 10:30); rather, destroy all of them, with all their altars, groves, and

images. That Israel did not carefully obey these orders brought them much distress throughout their history (e.g. Josh. 9:18; cf. 23:12–13).

6. *Hospitality to strangers*. Apart from the Canaanites, this ethnic segregation was not so strict that no foreigners could ever be present in Israel. The stranger and sojourner was recognized and protected (Deut. 10:18–19), could be circumcised and keep the Passover (Ex. 12:48), and could live as a servant in an Israelite home (Lev. 25:45; Ex. 12:45). Scripture highly values hospitality to strangers (e.g. Job 31:32; Gen. 19:2; Matt. 25:35), as should we. However, none of the cited passages dissolve the distinction between native and alien, but rather assume and affirm it. True hospitality, whether in a home or in a nation, never requires the dissolution of the boundaries between one people and another.

7. *Assimilation of foreigners*. However, in nations today there is a way in which certain foreigners can become, not mere sojourners, but more organic members of the people, namely by assimilation or naturalization. Was this true in ancient Israel? It appears this could happen in least in some respect by marriage: through her first husband, then through Boaz, Ruth the Moabitess gained certain legal standing in Israel (Ruth 1:4, 16; 4:5, 10) and became an ancestor of King David (4:17). Perhaps it could also happen in other ways, though whether and how is not always clear: for example, was David's mighty man Uriah the Hittite (2 Sam. 23:39) a resident foreign soldier, or a naturalized Israelite? And either

way, how was he granted an exception to the ban on Canaanites?

In whatever way strangers may have been assimilated, it is clear that it was not without restrictions, even those that were racially specific: "An Ammonite or Moabite shall not enter into the congregation of the LORD; even to their tenth generation... because they met you not with bread and with water in the way, when ye came forth out of Egypt" (Deut. 23:3–4). Compare verses 7–8, "Thou shalt not abhor an Edomite; for he is thy brother: thou shalt not abhor an Egyptian; because thou wast as stranger in his land. The children that are begotten of them shall enter into the congregation of the LORD in their third generation." It is not the place here to explain exactly what these laws meant and how they were applied: it is enough to underline that the Israelite nation had, by God's design, race-realist immigration policies.

8. *Intra-ethnic marriage.* We mentioned Boaz and Ruth, who were not the only ethnically-mixed married couple in Scripture (cf. e.g. Moses and Zipporah, Ex. 2:16, 21, and Joseph and Asenath, Gen. 41:50). So there was some legal provision for the recognition of such marriages. However, this should be recognized with the following clarifications.

First, not every example of the choices of Old Testament believers is approved merely because it is recorded in Scripture, nor is passive civil toleration itself a proof that all such marriages were strictly legal. Israel often enough ignored its righteous laws.

Second, the examples of mixed marriages in Scripture may be "inter-ethnic," but are not all "inter-racial" by our modern terms: Ruth's ancestor Moab was the son of Abraham's nephew Lot (Gen. 19:37), and Zipporah's father was a priest of Midian (Ex. 2:16, 21), Midian being a son of Abraham himself by Keturah (Gen. 25:2). It seems mostly likely that Moses' "Ethiopian" (in Hebrew, "Cushite") wife whom Miriam and Aaron complain about (Num. 12:1) is Zipporah herself, called a Cushite because "Cush" was sometimes used as name for the region in which the Midianites lived.

Third, even noting all exceptions, the vast majority of marriages recorded in the Scripture take place within the narrow confines of one nation, or even one tribe (see e.g. Chron. 1–9).

Fourth, certain foreign marriages were explicitly forbidden in the civil law (as with the Canaanites, Deut. 7:3), to the extent that some were legally annulled even after they were contracted (as in Ezra 10:2–3, 19), perhaps even after they were consummated (as appears from v. 44).

Fifth, certain specific persons were explicitly forbidden from choosing foreign spouses. The high priest could only marry "a virgin of his own people" (Lev. 21:14; cf. Ezek. 44:22). It is reasonable to think Deuteronomy 17:15 imposed similar requirements upon the king by good and necessary consequence: contrast the disaster of Solomon's foreign wives (1 Kings 11). Moreover, for the daughters of Zelophehad, the LORD's command was, "Let them marry to whom they think best; only to the family of the tribe of their father shall they marry. So shall not the inheritance of the children of Israel remove from tribe to tribe" (Num. 36:6–7). This last restriction is instructive, teaching that marriage, though a matter of personal choice, still is not thereby permitted to harm familial, tribal, or national interests. Moreover, it appears that laws against miscegenation cannot be unrighteous in themselves, as the righteous God did institute them in these cases.

We will discuss racially-mixed marriages again in the application chapter, but here we would highlight the zeal of Abraham in seeking a wife for his son from his kindred, though they lived far away (Gen. 24:3–4), Isaac's imitation of the same (Gen. 28:1–2), and the joy of Laban in finding a potential son-in-law in Jacob, "Surely thou art my bone and my flesh" (Gen. 29:14). Compare Adam's joy expressed in much the same way when he first saw Eve, after she was made from his own side (2:23).

In light of all these things, if some would assert that race realism in general, or in specific a preference for intra-ethnic or intra-racial marriage, is unique to the Old Testament economy, and not at all a matter of universal, permanent, general equity, we would simply say here, the burden of proof for this assertion rests entirely on them.

III: New Testament

The New Testament of course does not, and cannot, overturn the moral teaching of the Old, nor need it be repeated to remain in force. "One jot or one tittle shall in no wise pass from the law" (Matt. 5:17–18). We add here only a few brief new considerations.

1. *Incarnation.* Jesus Christ, the Lord of glory, took on a true human nature, and in this nature, like all men, he had a race, nation, tribe, and family. Moreover, none of these was chosen arbitrarily, but with great purpose, that he would be "made of the seed of David according to the flesh" (Rom. 1:3; 2 Sam. 7:12 with Ps. 110:1). Thus Matthew and Luke both feature genealogies of Christ. It will suffice to say here, those who use religion to dismiss race as irrelevant, cannot understand this matter well.

2. *Salvation.* There was provision for salvation of all nations in the Old Testament (e.g. Ex. 12:48), but the international character of true religion was made more clear under the New (Matt. 28:19). However, nothing about salvation changes a man's race, or its natural importance. Indeed, we have already seen that national distinctions will remain in heaven (Rev. 5:9; cf. 21:24), and thus it stands to reason they remain on earth, even in the church. Noteworthy in this respect is the question of the salvation of the presently apostate Jews. Together with many Christians I look forward

to a day when they will be engrafted back in their own olive tree (Rom. 11:23). Few confess, however, that this perspective *assumes* race realism. If the Jewish race is not real, it certainly cannot have promises made concerning it.

3. *Duty.* A special love for kin and nation is a part of natural affection. No one needs Scripture to know he ought to have such love (cf. Eph. 5:29). However, Scripture does explicitly affirm it, by the fifth commandment, "Honour thy father and thy mother" (Ex. 20:12), by Paul's example of compassion for his unbelieving "kinsmen according to the flesh" (Rom. 9:3), and by sharply rebuking those who are so degenerate as to be "without natural affection" (Rom. 1:31; 2 Tim. 3:3), especially within the church: "But if any provide not for his own, and specially for those of his own house, he hath denied the faith, and is worse than an infidel" (1 Tim. 5:8). A few moments of thought on what this means in our day, when the majority of professed Christians utterly despise race realism, should make the godly weep with Jeremiah (Jer. 9:1–3).

4. *Silence.* Finally, the New Testament says nothing to reverse the race realism evident in the Old Testament. The Bible simply is not "anti-racist." This negative could be disproven by one counter-example; however, having explored the Scriptures, we have not found a single one. This is perhaps the strongest argument of all. If Scripture defines sin as transgression of the law (1 John 3:4), and no law can be produced which race realism is proven to transgress, then it is

simply not a sin, and every moral objection to it falls down of its own accord.

We could address further objections here, but it seemed better to wait for chapter 5: Objections.

To summarize what we have said, the Bible teaches that race is real. Yes, race is a natural reality, and Scripture a supernatural book. However, this should be no barrier to hearing what it says on race. Indeed, as the Holy Scriptures are given to make men wise unto salvation (2 Tim. 3:15–17), we ought to receive their teaching with all the more reverence and urgency, even when they tell us earthly things (cf. John 3:12).

Chapter 3:
Nature

In the previous section on Scripture, we saw that God's Word teaches that race is real: by God's creation and providence, by the civil law of Moses, and also by the New Testament. We now turn from the book of Scripture to behold the book of nature, but as we do, we should remember that God wrote them both, and he cannot ever contradict himself in any way. Nature cannot ever contradict the truths of Scripture, and where nature can, it will corroborate Scripture. The same vice versa.

What we will do in this chapter is often called "noticing." We notice the reality of race, observing facts with our senses and drawing conclusions from those facts with our reason. We intend to appeal to common sense, but also will use statistics and science, not to oppose common sense, but to confirm it somewhat more rigorously. The main assumption behind this chapter is that readers can trust their natural knowledge and experience regarding race.

Nature is not lying to you.

I: The Body

First among natural racial realities are those that concern the body. The most immediately obvious is skin color. Everyone on earth fairly easily fits into the categories of "white," "brown," or "black" by skin color alone. Racial classifications can be more narrow than this, but they are still color-bound: northeast Asians are very light brown ("yellow"). Sub-Saharan Africans are very dark brown ("black"). Europeans are relatively pale ("white"). These colors are essential to these races: there is no such thing as a black member of the European race, or a white Sub-Saharan. Exceptions by mere geography don't count: e.g. Afrikaners in South Africa are European by race. Nor do diseases take away this distinction: e.g. an albino Kenyan would have normally had black skin.

Skin color is important, but race is much more than skin. Eye and hair color also have strong racial specificity. Blue eyes are far less common outside the European race, and even less so red hair. Facial structure strikingly differs among races: this is another way in which the albino Kenyan would still be rightly identified as Black. Medically, racial difference is more significant than most realize. Certain diseases occur mostly in one race, like sickle-cell anemia among Blacks. Forensic anthropologists can tell a person's race from just his skeleton. It appears there are even bodily features unknown to us by which computers can distinguish race. This article[22] summarizes a fascinating 2022 study:[23]

> Using imaging data of chest X-rays, limb X-rays, chest CT scans, and mammograms, the team trained a deep learning model to identify race as white, Black, or Asian — even though the images themselves contained no explicit mention of the patient's race. This is a feat even the most seasoned physicians cannot do, and it's not clear how the model was able to do this...
>
> To investigate possible mechanisms of race detection, they looked at variables like differences in anatomy, bone density, resolution of images — and many more, and the models still prevailed with high ability to detect race from chest X-rays. "These results were initially confusing, because the members of our research team could not come anywhere close to identifying a good proxy for this task," says paper co-author Marzyeh Ghassemi, ... "Even when you filter medical images past where the images are recognizable as medical images at all, deep models maintain a very high performance."

Moreover, inside our body's cells, behind all the differences we see, is the unseen genetic code received by combination of the genes of our racial ancestors. Modern science is able to map differences in genes directly today by sequencing, and

---

22 Rachel Gordon, "Artificial intelligence predicts patients' race from their medical images," MIT News, May 20, 2022: https://news.mit.edu/2022/artificial-intelligence-predicts-patients-race-from-medical-images-0520

23 Judy Wawira Gichoya MD, et al, "AI recognition of patient race in medical imaging: a modelling study," The Lancet Digital Health, June 2022: https://www.thelancet.com/journals/landig/article/PIIS2589-7500(22)00063-2/fulltext

this strongly confirms that our common racial classifications are real. In fact, "cluster analysis" maps genetic differences in a way that closely mirrors common racial classifications based on geography. The following two graphics are from the book *Human Diversity* by Charles Murray (pp. 151–52).[24] How they were produced is explained in the book, but the results are quite striking even without explanation:

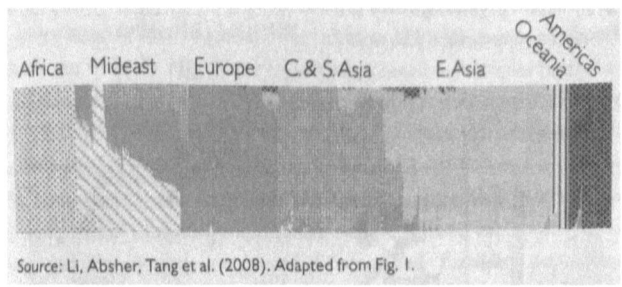

Source: Li, Absher, Tang et al. (2008). Adapted from Fig. 1.

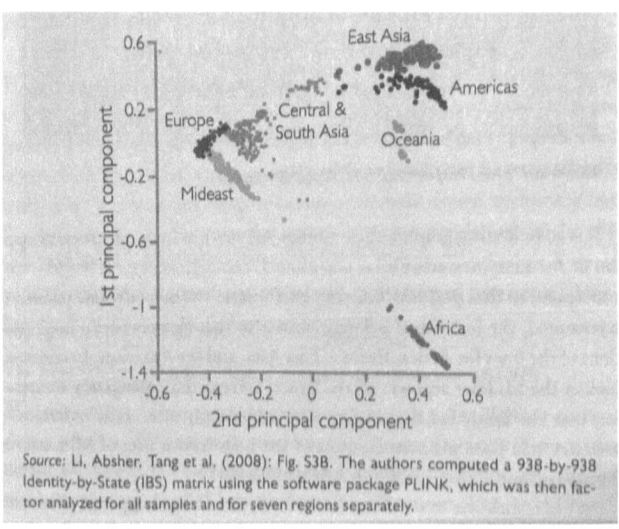

Source: Li, Absher, Tang et al. (2008): Fig. S3B. The authors computed a 938-by-938 Identity-by-State (IBS) matrix using the software package PLINK, which was then factor analyzed for all samples and for seven regions separately.

---

24   Charles Murray, *Human Diversity: The Biology of Gender, Race, and Class,* Twelve, 2020.

Of course, it should surprise no one that geographically isolated races also have isolated genes. What is surprising is, that against all common sense and science, church leaders have publicly declared the opposite, that race "has no biological reality."

II: Language

Races also differ by language. How people speak is not in the abstract a racial difference—a White businessman can become fluent in Chinese—but in the concrete almost always is, especially as concerns one's own native tongue. Europeans have European languages, most of which are closely related, and the same for northeast Asians and their languages. Language families not only reflect racial distinctions: in some ways they also cause them, because language barriers naturally increase genetic isolation: remember Babel. The close connection of race and language is why language families can bear racial names, e.g. Arabic is a Semitic language, and English an Indo-European language. Even within one language, dialect is often a decided racial boundary-marker. Even the hearing of brief phrases in a racial dialect immediately identifies a race, and brings to mind a host of non-linguistic differences: case in point, "I *axed* you a question."

III: Culture

"Culture" may seem inappropriate to mention here, because it is so broad a term, and many times it is in fact contrasted with race: "It's their culture, not their race." But as with language, any honest observer can see that different races have their different cultures that distinguish them. "White culture" is real, and anti-White hatred of it assumes this reality, as this poster put out in 2021 by the Smithsonian National Museum of African American History and Culture shows:

Religion
- Christianity is the norm
- Anything other than Judeo – Christian tradition is foreign
- No tolerance for deviation from single god concept

Status, Power & Authority
- Wealth = worth
- Your job is who you are
- Respect authority
- Heavy value on ownership of goods, space, property

Future Orientation
- Plan for future
- Delayed gratification
- Progress is always best
- "Tomorrow will be better"

Time
- Follow rigid time schedules
- Time viewed as a commodity

Aesthetics
- Based on European culture
- Steak and potatoes; "bland is best"
- Woman's beauty based on blonde, thin – "Barbie"
- Man's attractiveness based on economic status, power, intellect

Holidays
- Based on Christian religions
- Based on white history & male leaders

Justice
- Based on English common law
- Protect property & entitlements
- Intent counts

Competition
- Be #1
- Win at all costs
- Winner/loser dichotomy
- Action Orientation
- Master and control nature
- Must always "do something" about a situation
- Aggressiveness and Extroversion
- Decision-Making
- Majority rules (when Whites have power)

Communication
- "The King's English" rules
- Written tradition
- Avoid conflict, intimacy
- Don't show emotion
- Don't discuss personal life
- Be polite

"Black culture" is also real: consider the highly distinct music, performed by Blacks, that is available for listening on "Black Entertainment Television." "Asian culture" is also real, which is why "China Town" and Chinese restaurants are much the same in every major city in America. And so on.

Moreover, for a man of one race to try to cross over to another highly distinct race's culture is strange and irregular, sometimes resulting in humor, but often in social disapproval: Blacks generally despise the "Oreo," the Black who is perceived as trying to conform to Whites.

Specifics of culture that vary by race include family structure, living conditions, social norms, view of time, attitude toward work, choices of recreational activities, and food and drink. To give some examples: in 2022,[25] 63% of Black children in the United States had only one parent in the home, but only 24% of White children. White people like to hike, and to greet each other while hiking, and a video of Blacks making fun of this[26] went viral last year. Mexican Mestizos eat tacos, and White Americans eat burgers. Yes, both may enjoy the others' cuisine, but this does not disprove the racial character of food: in America tacos are served at a Mexican restaurant, and in Mexico burgers are served at an American restaurant. The reader can readily think of other examples that show how culture is strongly tied to race, which again demonstrates that races are real, and really different.

---

25 https://datacenter.aecf.org/data/tables/107-children-in-single-parent-families-by-race-and-ethnicity#detailed/1/any/false/1095,2048,1729,37,871,870,573,869,36,868/8223,4040,4039,2638,2597,4758,1353/432,431

26 Elyse Wanshel, "A Lighthearted TikTok About 'White People On A Hike' Became Weirdly Controversial," HuffPost, October 4, 2023: https://www.huffpost.com/entry/a-lighthearted-tiktok-about-white-people-on-a-hike-became-weirdly-controversial_n_651dbf68e4b00eb6fb38f62b

IV: Morality

Inseparable from culture, indeed one of its most important aspects, is morality. This bothers people to admit, but all know that it's true: distinct races have their distinct virtues and vices, for which they are well-known, as much as for their bodily and linguistic features. Usually the vices are more well-known than the virtues. For example, in 2021, Blacks made up 12.1% of the population living in the United States, but they committed 64% of the murders.[27] The same article just cited carefully argues that the greater criminality of Blacks is not because of differences in income from Whites, and it draws this conclusion: "All else being equal in terms of household income during adolescence, Black men are four times as likely to find themselves behind bars as White men." This is the secret reason violent crime rates are so high in America, and especially in the South: it's not our guns, it's our Blacks. Accordingly, state homicide rates correlate closely with the Black share of the population.[28]

But we reiterate, statistics should be used here as a confirmation of common sense. Perhaps Americans living in a White rural enclave in Vermont will need facts and figures to discern these truths, but urbanites and Southerners with daily experience of Blacks don't need to examine a chart to know they should avoid the Black part of town, especially at night.

---

27   Steve Sailer, "America's Black Male Problem," *Taki's Magazine*, February 15, 2023.
28   Steve Sailer, "The Geography of Homicide," *Taki's Magazine*, August 24, 2023.

Just as no experienced traveler needs to be told to book a vacation in Switzerland rather than Zimbabwe.

I focus on Black sins here because they're the most well-known, but oddly nonetheless least likely to be mentioned publicly. When it comes to Blacks, speaking of race-linked morality is highly taboo. One reason for this is that honest recognition of it would destroy the apparent justice of the "Civil Rights" narrative at the heart of modern leftism.

But some sensitive Christians will complain here, noting that sin is a moral, not a racial problem. Sin is a matter of the soul, not of the body. Race is genetic, morality is spiritual. The answer is, like language, morality is distinct from race in the abstract, but in many respects still inseparable from it in the concrete. Blacks, Whites, and Asians act in Black, White, and Asian ways, for good or ill. Moreover, yes morality is a matter of the soul, but the soul has a race as much as the body. Better said, the whole man has a race, and his body and soul are his two essential parts, the soul the informing form of the body, with each soul created uniquely by God for each body—this is the opinion of the creationists; traducianists teach the soul is procreated by the parents, so in that view also the soul properly has a race. And of course, the soul in doing good or evil usually employs the body, and is influenced by it.

Now, man the creature alone is the author of his sin. God does no moral evil, nor can he create or approve of it. But as daily experience with our own selves will show, our original spiritual corruption takes the diverse positive goods of our created constitution, and the diverse sorrowful evils of affliction and misery (God's just punishment for sin), and abuses them for the shameful evils of transgression in an analogously diverse way. Another way to say this is, like individual men, man's individual races have their individual besetting sins.

Consider also the well-known fact that offspring mimic their parents in both vice and virtue. That the same happens on a larger scale in entire races should surprise no one: races are highly extended families.

Now, as to exactly how morality is transmitted and impacted by race, and to what extent nature and nurture plays a role, and exactly how body and soul, genes and virtues, interact in moral actions, we need not explore here. It doesn't matter, really, for our proof that one of the distinguishing features of the races are the ways in which they each uniquely manifest a moral character.

V: Religion

We cannot mention morality without mentioning religion and piety, which properly considered are the chief part of morality. And the races certainly do differ in religion. Race and religion are hard to separate, so much so that some have the same name: "Turk" and "Hindu" in the past denoted both nations and religions. Today "Jew" does the same. Other religious names naturally join those of race in close association: "White Anglo-Saxon Protestant," for example, or "Irish Catholic," or "Arab Muslim."

Even today nations are called by their religion, or their past religion. The nations of historic Christendom in Europe, America, and Australia are sometimes still called "Christian nations," despite their widespread godlessness and secularism.

Even in lands identified as "Christian," ethno-religious differences are clear. If in one Sunday an impartial observer should attend two Protestant churches in one American city, one church White, the other Black, the difference he would observe would likely be greater than if he compared two services held on distinct continents, yet in churches made up of the same race.

Of course, a man's religion can change while his race remains the same. An entire race can even change its religion: the White ancestors of Christendom were all once pagan. But in all honesty, such change is rare. Most everyone remains his entire life in the religion of his people. For example, few Blacks today will ever join the historic, orthodox Reformed and Lutheran churches in America. Those churches are nearly as White today as they were in Europe during the Reformation. And on the rare occasion that Blacks do join such churches, they tend to prove the close association of race and religion, either by suffering as social outcasts from their race because of their religious choices, or by trying to remake their new religion to be more amenable to the distinct religion of their race: for example, by persuading White

Christians to praise Black preaching as better than that of Whites.

This is not at all to assert that it is impossible for non-Whites to embrace the orthodox Christianity of historic European Protestantism. But it does mean the barriers to this are higher than most recognize, and that we can hope for no success unless we reckon honestly with racial difference, even in religion.

VI: Intelligence

We move from racial differences in morality and religion to those which are evident in intelligence. For this again experience is a better teacher than statistics, but it will help readers if we present clear data. In doing this we must briefly explain IQ. A person's "intelligence quotient" is a measure of his intellectual ability determined by tests that are rigorous and repeatable. IQ is strongly linked to success in parts of life that require the intelligence being measured, which is why IQ tests were used in evaluating potential employees, until the Supreme Court ruled this unconstitutional,[29] because Whites did better than Blacks on the tests.

Yes, certain races do get better scores on IQ tests than others. But it is false to attribute this to racial malice in the test-makers. A simpler and more correct explanation is that the tests are fine, and the results accurate, but they are

---

29   "Griggs v. Duke Power," North Carolina History Project, accessed February 3, 2025, https://northcarolinahistory.org/encyclopedia/griggs-v-duke-power/.

politically embarrassing. Scientists devoted to the study of intelligence and race assert that the tests produce highly reliable results. I cannot field all objections against IQ tests here, but they are ably dealt with in the introduction to Richard Herrnstein and Charles Murray's well-known book, *The Bell Curve*.[30]

So what do the tests reveal? That races are quite different in their intellectual capacity. Chapter 13 of *The Bell Curve* presents striking testimony to this, summarized in this IQ distribution (p. 279):

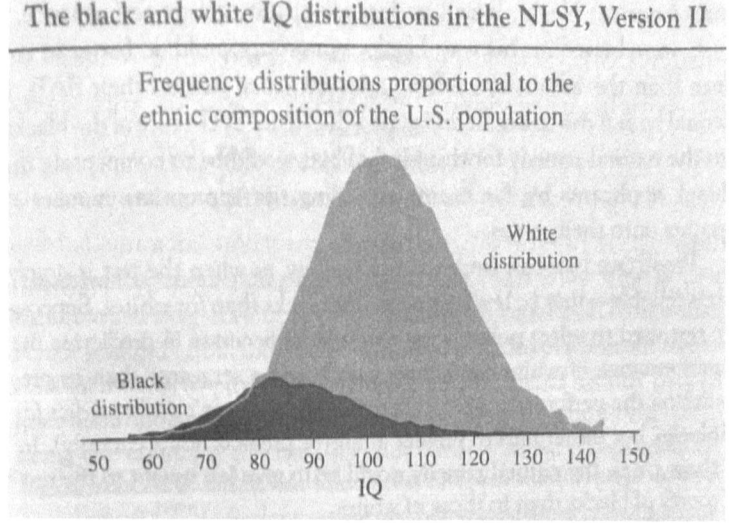

The black and white IQ distributions in the NLSY, Version II

Frequency distributions proportional to the ethnic composition of the U.S. population

This chart shows that in America, the average IQ of Whites is about 100, and that of Blacks, about 85. The difference amounts to what is called a "standard deviation," which

---

30 Richard J. Herrnstein and Charles Murray, *The Bell Curve: Intelligence and Class Structure in American Life*, Free Press, 1994.

means, "The average White person tests higher than about 84 percent of the population of Blacks and the average Black person tests higher than about 16 percent of the population of Whites" (p. 269). The authors go on to prove carefully that these data are not subject to bias, or skewed by socio-economic status (in fact, when status is higher, the Black-White intellectual divide is greater). Moreover, the tests are equally accurate in predicting intelligence-related outcomes in both races.

Let's consider the same chart above, adjusted for population size (p. 279):

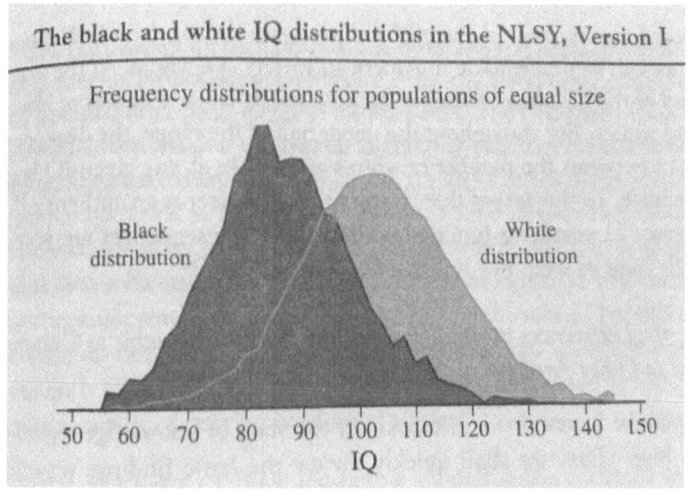

Note how on the right side of the chart, the number of Blacks dwindles to almost nothing around 120. 120 was the average IQ of physicians[31] in 2002. So what happens when initiatives

---

31 "Occupational IQ Estimates," IQ Comparison Site, accessed February 3, 2025, https://www.iqcomparisonsite.com/occupations.aspx.

for "Diversity, Equity, and Inclusion" push for more Black doctors, even though very few Blacks have the requisite intelligence for it? The standards of medical instruction will have to be lowered, to the harm of patients. "DEI means DIE" is an apt warning, which we ignore at our peril.

VII: Place

In addition to all the above is the fact that races differ in their places. This is true geographically. Not even modern mass immigration has dissolved God's appointed "bounds of their habitation" (Acts 17:26): as a rule, Whites live in Europe, North America, and Australia, Browns in North Africa, Asia, and South America, and Blacks in Sub-Saharan Africa. Moreover, in places where populations of diverse races happen to live in closer proximity, a similar geographical segregation usually occurs. In countless U.S. cities, Blacks, Whites, Latinos, and Chinese live in distinct parts of town, without legal coercion. Indeed for example, decades after legal segregation ended, the racial geographical divide is stark in Atlanta:[32]

---

32 Image here: https://x.com/___eb__/status/1806320840847601719

Mere geography aside, it is also true that races differ in their places in society. This is so in education: Blacks, Whites, and Asians tend to have distinct outcomes in learning. This is so in vocation: Blacks, Whites, and Asians tend to choose different careers. Just as some specific ethnicities are associated with certain types of work, at least in certain places: in my hometown, Greeks often ran the restaurants.

This is also true in politics. Again this is controversial, but the facts are clear. Certain races tend to rule, but others tend to be ruled. Since the time of the Romans, it is fair to say that Whites have exercised dominion above others in the world. Not always and everywhere of course, but in many times and places, and especially so in more recent years. The dreaded term "White supremacy" is an apt description of the latter course of history. Consider the vast British Empire, in which White men ruled a quarter of the world. Or consider the present American Empire, in which for good or ill, one White nation indisputably holds more global power than any other nation. This power need not be that of an official formal empire to be real. For example, rulers and businessmen of every race today wear Anglo-American-style formal suits, without legal coercion, because (as leftists correctly say), power and Whiteness are closely tied.

And on the other side, Black political subjection is also an undeniable reality. This is true in places they have lived together closely with Whites: e.g. under American slavery and segregation, and under South African Apartheid. These systems have fallen, but the basic relation of Black and White in America has changed little. Blacks as a whole today are clients of White and Jewish Democrats, obtaining welfare, free abortion, political preferment, and criminal immunity in exchange for blind loyalty to the Party. Whether this slavery is better than the former, the reader can decide.

Black political subjection appears even when they form their own governments: witness the steep descent into tyranny and anarchy after the Haitian revolution, and the same occurring presently under Black rule in South Africa. For similar examples, research the history of Liberia, and of Rhodesia turned Zimbabwe. Yes, White nations have had their own times of great turmoil, like the French Revolution, but these are not so much the rule as in Black nations. France itself has a long history of strong civil government, even rule over other distant nations. Nor can White colonization be blamed for the frequent political disasters in Black nations. White explorers found many Blacks in no better state than they are in today. For one proof of this, read this harrowing testimony of how the English found Benin City, Nigeria:

INSTITUTE OF CURRENT WORLD AFFAIRS

DER - 42   May 16, 1955
Notes on Nigeria - II   Malta

Mr. Walter S. Rogers
Institute of Current World Affairs
522 Fifth Avenue
New York 36, New York

Dear Mr. Rogers:

    Benin City lies to the west of the Niger and is near the sprawling delta of that mighty river. These days Benin is just another ramshackle Nigerian town, filled with mud-walled houses and tiny shops. But Benin is different from the others in its history. All of southern Nigeria was a land of oppression, terror and fiendish cruelty, of slave raids, slavery, juju, human sacrifice and cannibalism. But Benin surpassed them all as a City of Blood.

    Hundreds of people were tortured to death regularly in Benin's juju rituals. These blood-stained orgies went on for centuries, and were only halted in 1897 when the British captured the city. One man who entered the city in the British expedition gave this description:

    "...Altars covered with streams of dried human blood, the stench of which was awful... huge pits, forty to fifty feet deep, were found filled with human bodies, dead and dying, and a few wretched captives were rescued alive... everywhere sacrificial trees on which were the corpses of the latest victims---everywhere, on each path, were newly sacrificed corpses. On the principal sacrificial tree, facing the main gate of the King's compound, there were two crucified bodies..."*

Moreover, self-governing Black nations are not independent in the way White countries are. Like Blacks in American ghettos, foreign Blacks depend at least in part on handouts from the U.S. government, at the cost of about eight billion dollars annually.[33]

---

33   See the detailed report, "U.S. Assistance for Sub-Saharan Africa: An Overview," *Congressional Research Service*, accessed Feb. 4th: https://sgp.fas.org/crs/row/R46368.pdf

All of this to say, under the idea of place, speaking geographically, socially, and politically, the races have been set apart. They are divided by barriers as real, and in some ways as impassable, as the Sahara Desert.

VIII: Analogies

We have spoken of various observable matters that demonstrate the reality of race and racial difference. Our own senses and reason testify to race realism, and no man, especially no Christian man, should ever presume to deny the things that everyone can see. The Bible itself does not, indeed cannot, contradict empirical reality, for the Creator cannot contradict himself. No wonder then that many things said in this chapter confirm the things said in the previous. Scripture and nature never disagree, and when they speak of the same things, they speak in harmony.

Assuming the facts above, we conclude this chapter with two analogies to other natural things that will help readers better understand the natural reality of race.

First, the various human races are like parts or members of one body. Man is an organic whole, united by one blood, despite all differences still obviously one race, one human species, distinguished from all other animals by his reasonable soul. But as in a body, relatively speaking, the several parts differ quite widely among themselves. Compare the foot and eye, the toe and mouth. Man's various sub-races or sub-species then are like these different parts: all human, and all valuable in their own place, yet quite diverse in shape, function, honor, and importance.

Moreover, as with physical bodies, disease can affect some parts more than others: some ethnic members of the human race are marked more than the rest by the disease of sin and its attendant misery, some to the point that they are nearly rotting away. To put it another way, though all races are born dead in sin, some are in certain regards degenerate beyond the rest, notably bereft of natural virtues and affections that remain in other parts. "The Cretians are alway liars, evil beasts, slow bellies" (Titus 1:12). This should not surprise us any more than finding a malignant tumor in the spleen, but not the brain.

Some may object here that we are abusing an analogy that the apostle uses for the church (Rom. 12:4–5, I Cor. 12:12–27). But the analogy holds for mankind in general as well as for redeemed mankind specifically. Indeed, it holds in the church in part because churches are made up of men. Granted, Paul speaks primarily of spiritual endowments, and we are primarily addressing natural characteristics. But the analogy still holds. It is as true for human races as it is for Christian people: "God set the members every one of them in the body, as it hath pleased him" (1 Cor. 12:18), and to God's pleasure we should gladly assent and submit.

Second, mankind is like a tree, and its various racial classifications like its branches. There is one trunk from Adam and Noah, which splits into three major branches in

Japheth, Shem, and Ham, and from there by various forks into other divisions: from race, to nation, to tribe, to clan, to family. So yes, man is one tree, that is, one race, but that tree has many branches, which are still part of the tree, yet nonetheless are distinct from the trunk, and separate from the other branches, some of them quite distantly now after centuries of growth.

Of course this analogy breaks down, as human branches can recombine, and have done so through racial mixing: tree branches naturally stay separate. But even here, the analogy can still be useful. In certain plants one branch can indeed be set into another branch, and this union can produce growth and fruit. But this rarely happens spontaneously: grafting is artificial. Moreover, it requires wounding both branches, which brings risk of disease and failure. And what is more, we ought to question the assertion of a sovereign right to "graft" men's races into one another as a farmer does with trees. Men are not plants.

These analogies and the facts that they presume have much to teach us about relations among the races of mankind. But before considering application, we will turn next to consider history, and then to field common objections.

Chapter 4:
History

Introduction

Having considered what nature had to teach concerning race, we will now consider history, not as in the previous chapter simply to observe facts and draw conclusions from them, but here with a more normative purpose, i.e. that historical answers to questions of race might better help us answer the same questions today.

History is vast, and our knowledge and space limited, so of the many studies that could have been illuminating in this matter, we have chosen to narrow our scope to the history of the United States of America. We will first look at an overview of this history, and then focus on the opinions of certain Christians who lived at various points in it.

I: The History of Race in America

From well before their independence the thirteen American colonies were decidedly White. They were ruled by White Britain, and the large majority of their population were native English, with a minority of various other Whites, especially Scots and Irish, but also Dutch, French, German, and Swedish. This White population recognized and defended a firm contrast between themselves and racial minorities that lived near and among them, namely American Indians, and African slaves.

We will look at the relationship with Indians, but will specifically focus on the Africans. They were subject to the Whites as their slaves, and the small population of freed Blacks joined the slaves in a similar subordinate relation to the White population. The relation between the races was clearly and distinctly that of superior and inferior, and this relation was strictly maintained by law.

Consider for example, "An act for the better preventing of a spurious and mixed issue," passed in Massachusetts in 1705, which contained two provisions. First,

> If any negro or mulatto shall presume to smite or strike any person of the English or other Christian nation, such negro or mulatto shall be severely whipped, at the discretion of the justices before whom the offender shall be convicted.

And second,

> None of her Majesty's English or Scottish subjects, nor of any other Christian nation, within this province, shall contract matrimony with any negro or mulatto; nor shall any person, duly authorised to solemnize marriage, presume to join any such in marriage, on pain of forfeiting the sum of fifty pounds.

As to the second provision, such marriage laws were by no means isolated, rare, or short-lived in America. The first laws against miscegenation or race-mixing in marriage were set in place in the colonies as early as the 1660s. Eventually the large majority of the present U.S. states enacted them, and most were not overturned until the 20th century.[34]

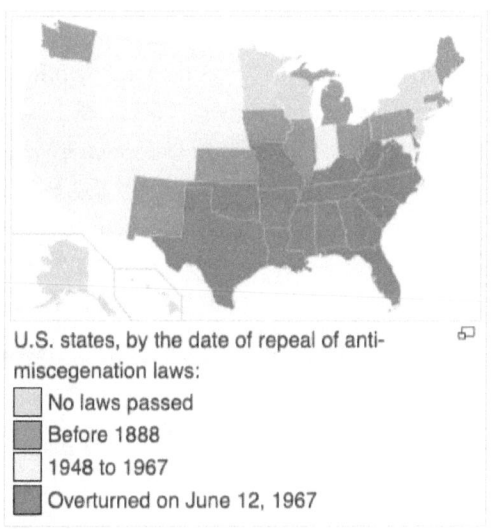

U.S. states, by the date of repeal of anti-miscegenation laws:

- ☐ No laws passed
- ■ Before 1888
- ☐ 1948 to 1967
- ■ Overturned on June 12, 1967

---

34 Graphic here: https://en.wikipedia.org/wiki/Anti-miscegenation_laws_in_the_United_States#:~:text=In%201967%2C%20the%20United%20States,marriage%20was%20Alabama%20in%202000.

When the colonies sought independence from Britain, the relation between Whites and Blacks did not change. Many make much of the phrase in the 1776 Declaration of Independence, "All men are created equal," but this cannot be interpreted as a statement of racial egalitarianism. Consider the explanation of it given in the 1857 Supreme Court ruling, Dred Scott v. Sandford,[35] which declared that Blacks were not, nor intended to be, citizens of the United States:

> It is too clear for dispute, that the enslaved African race were not intended to be included, and formed no part of the people who framed and adopted this declaration; for if the language, as understood in that day, would embrace them, the conduct of the distinguished men who framed the Declaration of Independence would have been utterly and flagrantly inconsistent with the principles they asserted...
>
> They perfectly understood the meaning of the language they used, and how it would be understood by others; and they knew that it would not in any part of the civilized world be supposed to embrace the negro race, which by common consent, had been excluded from civilized Governments... The unhappy black race were separated from the white by indelible marks, and laws long before established.

The 1789 U.S. Constitution confirms this interpretation. In it, "We the people," represented entirely by White signatories, established the constitutional government in order to "secure the blessings of liberty to ourselves and our posterity," which

---

35   "Dred Scott v. Sandford (1857)," National Archives, accessed February 3, 2025, https://www.archives.gov/milestone-documents/dred-scott-v-sandford.

posterity naturally would all be White. Moreover, America's first immigration law, the Naturalization Act of 1790,[36] clearly enforced the nation's White identity, as a candidate for naturalization was required to be, besides "a person of good character," also "a free white person."

As is well-known, relations between Whites and Blacks in America began to change in the 19th century. Though Virginia preceded any Northern state, and also Britain, in abolishing the slave trade, Black slavery itself was more widely used and defended in the South. This became a notable occasion for Southern secession in 1861, and the bloody war that followed. The conquest by the North in 1865 meant the immediate abolition of slavery (in the 13th Amendment), and an ensuing lengthy effort to make the legal status of Blacks equal to that of Whites, in the passing of the Civil Rights Act (1866), the 14th Amendment declaring "all persons born or naturalized" in the U.S. to be citizens (1868), and the 15th Amendment forbidding disenfranchisement "on account of race, color, or previous condition of servitude" (1870). Compared to what we saw above, these changes were a total revolution for race relations in America, at least in terms of civil law.

The process of attempting to impose this new legal racial order upon the South, called Reconstruction, was not entirely successful. The South resisted by passing the so-called "Jim Crow" laws as early as the 1870s. These laws provided for

---

36 United States Statutes at Large, vol. 1, 1st Cong., 2nd sess., ch. 3, accessed February 3, 2025,
https://en.wikisource.org/wiki/United_States_Statutes_at_Large/Volume_1/1st_Congress/2nd_Session/Chapter_3.

various forms of legal segregation between Whites and Blacks, and they were upheld under the provision "separate but equal" in the 1896 Supreme Court case *Plessy v. Ferguson*.

But the egalitarian revolution was by no means over. Decades of agitation against the remnant of historic American race realism ensued, which resulted in the end of legal segregation. This happened officially in public schools by the 1954 Supreme Court case *Brown v. Board of Education of Topeka*, and despite years of coordinated "Massive Resistance" that followed, it was eventually imposed by force. This was notably evident in the Ole Miss Riot of 1962, in which President Kennedy sent 30,000 troops to enforce the enrollment of the first Black student at the University of Mississippi. The remnants of legal segregation were then dismantled by the Civil Rights Acts of 1964 and the Voting Rights Act of 1965. And to bring our history full circle, the three-hundred-year history of laws against inter-racial marriage in America was ended by the 1967 Supreme Court decision *Loving v. Virginia*.

II: Christian Race Realism in America

The facts above should not be a matter of dispute, but how they ought to be interpreted has been a source of continual controversy. In this controversy we maintain that the right and Christian view was that originally held at our nation's founding, embraced by its majority White and Christian population, and reflected in its laws, some of which we saw persisted for centuries, even through enormous political upheavals.

We have already made arguments from Scripture and nature for this opinion, and we intend soon to clear it from objections and apply it further. But here we want to call upon the testimony of historic Christians in America in order to confirm it. We will consider six men over four centuries, and will find them speaking largely with one voice.

John Eliot (c. 1604–1690), an English Puritan who moved to Boston, earned the name "Apostle to the Indians" for his diligent mission work among the Algonquians. He painstakingly learned the Massachusett language, adapted it to a written alphabet, wrote a grammar for it, and translated the entire Bible into it. The Lord blessed his labors, and he was able to establish for the "praying Indians," not only their own churches, but also their own towns, fourteen in number, the government of which, by Eliot's instruction, was based on Exodus 18.

We would note two things from this example. First, such labors presume real inequality between the White man and the Indian. If this were not the case, it would be the height of arrogance for a White missionary to cross an ocean, settle in a wilderness, and insist on teaching its inhabitants an entirely new religion, as well as an entirely new civil polity. However, Eliot was not arrogant. Rather, he was kind, full of compassion, and of faith in Jesus Christ, who came to save lost sinners. Cotton Mather expresses the national inequality which was presumed in this international mission when he praises Eliot's love and faith:[37]

> To think of raising a number of these hideous creatures unto the elevations of our holy religion, must argue more than common or little sentiments in the undertaker; but the faith of an Eliot could encounter it.

Second, Eliot's labors to serve another race did not require the mixing of his own race with theirs. He judged it best to keep the praying Indians separate, not only ecclesiastically, but also geographically and politically. We note that the same Eliot in 1689 did stipulate in a donation to a school in Roxbury that it should instruct the town's White children "together with such negroes or Indians as may or shall come."[38] But this does not necessarily oppose race realism. Better taken, it underlines a point we will make later, that prudent maintenance of racial difference does not require the same form of racial segregation in every circumstance.

The famous preacher and theologian *Jonathan Edwards* (1703–1758) himself also served for a few years as a missionary to Indians. But we would focus here on how he considered African slaves (a topic considered from an

---

37 Martin Moore, *Memoirs of the Life and Character of Rev. John Eliot, Apostle to the N.A. Indians*, 1822, p18.
   https://archive.org/details/memoirslifeandc00goog/page/n23/mode/2up

38 "Eliot School: In Session Here Since 1676," Jamaica Plain Historical Society, archived January 22, 2017, accessed February 3, 2025, https://web.archive.org/web/20170122214932/http://www.jphs.org/colonial/eliot-school-in-session-here-since-1676.html.

egalitarian perspective by Richard Anderson elsewhere).[39] Edwards' parents owned one slave, and Edwards himself owned more than one. He wrote a brief defense of a local fellow minister whose congregation was denouncing him for slave-owning. In his other writings we see various qualifications of his use and defense of African slavery: that the slave trade itself was condemnable for its cruelty, and that Europeans and Africans, though not temporal equals, are equally to be called to faith in Christ, who as the Savior of sinners from all nations, "Condescends to poor negroes." In proof of this his congregation in Northampton did admit nine Africans to full communicant membership, together with some Indians, again showing that even in a context where distinctions among races are recognized and legally enforced, prudence does not require entire racial separation in every sphere, in every circumstance.

In coming to the 19th century we meet the Southern Presbyterians. Many know the godly testimony of the praying Presbyterian deacon and war hero, General Thomas "Stonewall" Jackson. We will speak here of two ministers who were prominent in his Presbyterian church. First is *James Henley Thornwell* (1812–1862), renowned preacher, theologian, professor, president of South Carolina College, and defender of the Southern Presbyterians in debates over ecclesiology with Princeton Seminary professor Charles Hodge.

---

39 "Jonathan Edwards," *Princeton & Slavery*, accessed February 3, 2025, https://slavery.princeton.edu/stories/jonathan-edwards#ref-12.

Relevant to the topic of race, we commend his sermon "The Rights and Duties of Masters,"[40] preached in 1850 at the dedication of church building erected in Charleston, S.C. "for the benefit and instruction of the coloured population," as well as his "Report on Slavery,"[41] written in light of the growing international opposition to Southern slavery, for "explaining the position of Southern Christians, and vindicating their right to the confidence, love, and fellowship of all who everywhere call upon the name of our common Master." In these he not only speaks on race and slavery, but also condemns abolitionism as a form of atheism, spelling the ruin of all true religion and good government.

Passing by those works, here we will focus on the "Address of the Presbyterian Church in the Confederate States of America to All the Churches of Jesus Christ Throughout the Earth",[42] which Thornwell penned, and which was adopted unanimously as the manifesto of the newly founded PC (CSA), after it was forced to withdraw from its prior union with Northern Presbyterians, when their formerly united church required its ministers to profess loyalty to the Northern Federal government. As the Southern church was marked by slaveholding, the address includes a brief defense of the lawfulness of slavery, and the right of slaveholders to be church members without censure. It asks,

---

40 https://archive.org/details/rightsandduties00thorgoog/page/n6/mode/2up
41 https://archive.org/details/reportonsubjecto00pres/page/n5/mode/2up
42 See p531, here:
    https://static1.squarespace.com/static/590be125ff7c502a07752a5b/t/
    5fce9688c8da4936129da24b/1607374472329/
    Thornwell%2C+James+Henley%2C+Address+of+the+Presbyterian+Churc
    h+in+the+Confederate+States+to+all+the+Churches+of+Jesus+Christ.pdf

Shall our names be cast out as evil, and the finger of scorn pointed at us, because we utterly refuse to break our communion with Abraham, Isaac, and Jacob, with Moses, David, and Isaiah, with Apostles, Prophets, and Martyrs, with all the noble army of Confessors who have gone to glory from slave-holding countries and from a slave-holding Church, without ever having dreamed they were living in mortal sin, conniving at slavery in the midst of them? If so, we shall take consolation in the cheering consciousness that our Master has accepted us.

But closer to our purpose is its statement of the wholesome benefits for Africans themselves from the system of Southern slavery, namely that it brings them both salvation and civilization:

Indeed, as we contemplate their condition in the Southern States, and contrast it with that of their fathers before them, and that of their brethren, in the present day, in their native land, we cannot but accept it as a gracious Providence, that they have been brought in such numbers to our shores, and redeemed from the bondage of barbarism and sin. Slavery, to them, has certainly been over-ruled for the greatest good. It has been a link in the wondrous chain of Providence, through which many sons and daughters have been made heirs of the heavenly inheritance. The Providential result is, of course, no justification, if the thing is intrinsically wrong; but it is certainly a matter of devout thanksgiving, and no obscure intimation of the will and purpose of God, and of the consequent duty of the Church. We cannot forbear to say, however, that the general operation of the system is kindly and benevolent; it is a real and effective discipline, and without it, we are profoundly persuaded that the African race in the midst of us can never be elevated in the scale of being. As long as that race, in its comparative degradation, co-exists side by side with the white, bondage is its normal condition.

Note three important conclusions from this quote. First, the Southern Presbyterians gratefully recognized that slavery had been an occasion to the slaves themselves of enormous good, especially that of salvation. Second, they held out hope that Africans could be further Christianized and civilized under the benevolent tutelage of their White masters. But third, they knew until such racial improvement happened to a sufficient degree, the slavery of Blacks to Whites would remain a condition appropriate to the nature of both races.

We could say many things to introduce *Robert Lewis Dabney* (1820–1898), pastor, professor, polemicist, theologian, architect, and chief of staff to Stonewall Jackson. But it will suffice to allow B. B. Warfield (though no ally of Dabney on matters of race[43]) to praises his virtues:

Those who knew him best loved him most. His career was a distinguished one; his contributions to the theological sciences are of the first order; his services to the Presbyterian Churches are inestimable: may not only his memory remain green, but his influence be increased through the coming years!

---

43 See here: https://biblioskolex.wordpress.com/2021/12/11/may-his-memory-be-increased-benjamin-b-warfield-on-robert-lewis-dabney-and-race/

Among many other contributions, this distinguished theologian manfully defended race realism. A key work is his 1867 *Defence of Virginia,* in which he vindicates the recently defeated Southern cause in the matter of slavery, arguing at length from history, law, Old Testament, New Testament, ethics, and economics, and carefully demolishing objections, many of which are often raised today. Like Edwards did, he condemns the evils of the slave trade, while arguing that slavery itself is lawful, not just in the abstract, but in the concrete, in the lately abolished American slavery of Africans. And like Thornwell, Dabney condemns abolitionism as atheistic rebellion, akin to the Jacobinism of the French Revolution.

To touch directly on the racial teaching of the work, consider this prophetic warning from his conclusion, as to how the triumph of abolitionism will bring the calamitous dissolution of racial difference:

> Calhoun, and other Southern statesmen, with a sagacity which every day confirms, had forewarned us, that when once abolition by federal aggression came, these other sure results would follow: that the same greedy lust of power which had meddled between masters and slaves, would assuredly, and for the stronger reason, desire to use the political weight of the late slaves against their late masters: that having enforced a violent emancipation, they would enforce, of course, negro suffrage, negro eligibility to office, and a full negro equality: that negro equality thus theoretically established would be practical negro superiority: that the tyrant section, as it gave to its victims, the white men of the South, more and more causes of just

resentment, would find more and more violent inducements to bribe the negroes, with additional privileges and gifts, to assist them in their domination: that this miserable career must result in one of two things, either a war of races, in which the whites or the blacks would be, one or the other, exterminated; or amalgamation. But while we believe that "God made of one blood all nations of men to dwell under the whole heavens," we know that the African has become, according to a well-known law of natural history, by the manifold influences of the ages, a different, fixed species of the race, separated from the white man by traits bodily, mental and moral, almost as rigid and permanent as those of genus. Hence the offspring of an amalgamation must be a hybrid race, stamped with all the feebleness of the hybrid, and incapable of the career of civilization and glory as an independent race. And this apparently is the destiny which our conquerors have in view. If indeed they can mix the blood of the heroes of Manassas with this vile stream from the fens of Africa, then they will never again have occasion to tremble before the righteous resistance of Virginian freemen; but will have a race supple and vile enough to fill that position of political subjection, which they desire to fix on the South.[44]

Note his forceful articulation of points we have already made in our definition and defense of race realism. Note also his forceful application of them, in his rejection of miscegenation with disgust and horror. Modern egalitarians will hardly bear to read his words, and may call them the ravings of a

---

44 Robert L. Dabney, *A Defence of Virginia, and Through Her, of the South, in Recent and Pending Contests Against the Sectional Party*, E.J. Hale & Son, 1867, pp. 352–353.
(https://archive.org/details/defenceofvirgini00dabn/page/352/mode/2up)

madman. But they are not. They are the sober judgment of a pious theologian, representing the consensus of the hearts, the habits, and the laws of an entire Christian people.

To understand how Southerners applied these principles in church, it is worth noting another work by Dabney, a transcript of a speech he gave in 1867 to the Presbyterian Synod of Virginia, entitled "Ecclesiastical Relation of Negroes,"[45] or "Against the Ecclesiastical Equality of Negro Preachers in Our Church, and Their Right to Rule over White Christians." In it he applies a realistic assessment of the gifts of Blacks, and of the present extreme racial tensions following the war, asserting it would not be fitting for Black ministers to exercise rule over Whites in church, and moreover, that Black ministry to Whites would effectively communicate Black social equality with Whites, and would therefore lead to the unthinkable result of racial amalgamation. He also deals thoroughly with objections, especially those made from the spiritual unity in Christ of Black and White believers, which he affirms. His treatment of Galatians 3:28 (p. 12), a text often used by racial egalitarians today, is worthy of careful meditation. To give a good sense of the whole speech, we quote from his concluding summary (p. 15):

> The universality of gospel blessings to all believers does not carry with it a universal right to church office, as was asserted. God has often restrained the latter, on grounds of

---

45 Read here:
https://static1.squarespace.com/static/590be125ff7c502a07752a5b/t/5e3d9609c5fca0547a86b743/1581094411221/Dabney%2C+Robert+Lewis%2C+Ecclesiastical+Relation+of+Negroes.pdf

class, or natural distinction, where he has conceded the former. God has given to his church discretion to restrain it for similar cause, in suitable unrevealed instances. The Church has in every age exercised this lawful discretion, for her own general edification. The case of the negroes among us presents just such an instance, where the wise exercise of the scriptural discretion is proper. For, as I have shown, the setting up of black men to rule white Presbyterians, is, on every account, not for the church's true edification.[46]

Moreover, to see that in this matter he did not neglect the souls of Black men, but sincerely desired their spiritual good, consider his response to the question, "What alternative do you propose?":

I reply that I would first kindly invite and advise the black people to remain as they were, members of our churches, and under our instruction and church government. For I am well assured that this would prove best for their true interests. But if they will not be wise enough to agree to this, while I deplore their mistake, I would still attempt to do them all the good possible, which can be done without injustice to our church, and by righteous means. Then, as the second alternative, I would assist and encourage them to build up a black Presbyterian Church, ecclesiastically independent of, and separate from ours, but in relations of friendship and charity. To this end, I would extend to them ministerial and missionary labour liberally. I would aid them in church building. I would provide schools, separate from our own, for training black men to be pastors of black churches; and I would, if necessary, give ordination to enough men to form a separate Presbytery, when enough

---

46 Ibid., p16.

can be found possessed of constitutional qualifications. But I would make no black man a member of a white Session, or Presbytery, or Synod, or Assembly; nor would I give them any share in the government of our own church, nor any representation in it. 'It is confusion.'[47]

Now we confess that Dabney writes with great force and sharpness, and even some who are sympathetic to his principles will be put off by his words. To temper this somewhat, and to show the full picture of Southern Presbyterianism, we add two excerpts from *Rev. Ebenezer Thompson Baird* (1821–1887), from "The Religious Instruction of Our Coloured Population",[48] a pastoral letter to the churches of the Tombeckbee Presbytery. In it he movingly appeals to White masters to labor for the souls of their Black servants:

> Our servants are bone of our bone, and flesh of our flesh. The Saviour Jesus, who died for us, died for them. How can we love Christ, and yet be destitute of love for our servants; and how can you, who are masters, refuse to exert yourselves for their salvation? The older ones gathered around your cradles and welcomed you into the world with joy in your nestling infancy; the younger ones were the friends, the companions and playmates of your childhood— all of them have participated both in your joys and in your sorrows. When you have wept at the graves of your kindred,

---

47   Ibid., pp15-16.
48   See p345:
     https://static1.squarespace.com/static/590be125ff7c502a07752a5b/t/
     5f4542acb7e50d09e745ac3c/1598374572629/
     Baird%2C+Ebenezer+Thompson%2C+The+Religious+Instruction+of+Our
     +Colored+Population.pdf

they have wept with you; and when you shall be gathered to your fathers, among the sincerest mourners at your graves will be your own servants. How can you love Christ, and not love to give your servants, who are your best and most attached friends, the gospel of his love? And oh! how dare you think of that day and hour, when you shall be summoned yourselves by the Great Master, to give an account of your stewardship, and leave undone this most important part of your duty. And if it shall be so that, by God's great mercy, you shall yourselves be saved as by fire, how think you will you appear at the judgment seat, if it shall then be seen that your servants are lost through your default. Fearful, brethren, are the responsibilities of the master.

Baird, as Thornwell did above, also speaks movingly of how slavery has served the interests of both Whites and Blacks, and advanced their true spiritual unity in Christ:

But when we look for a single moment at the condition of our slaves, and compare it with what they were when they first came among us, barbarians and heathens from Africa, we are constrained to cry out: What hath not the Lord wrought for them? To-day they are as far superior to their savage ancestors as we are superior to them. So, also, this advancing civilization among them, sanctified by the spirit of Christianity, has done much to ameliorate the whole institution of slavery...

The master everywhere shows a more abiding interest in the true well-being of his servants; the servants exhibit a more trustful confidence in their master as their friend and protector. And so they go to the house of God together, learn their lessons of duty from the same Bible, rejoice in

the hopes of a common salvation, and gather together
around the table of the same Saviour.

We see in this that the Southern Presbyterians could at once
affirm racial difference, even deep racial inequality, and recoil
at any undue crossing of clear racial boundaries, yet at the
same time happily live, work, and worship with their Black
servants, labor for their temporal and eternal good, and enjoy
true unity and fellowship with them in Christ. These godly
men are an excellent historical example of Christian race
realism believed and applied, and for that they are worthy of
our study, and our honor.

We follow up on Thornwell and Dabney by introducing
two of their Presbyterian children in the 20th century. The
first is *J. Gresham Machen* (1881–1937), born in Baltimore,
professor of New Testament and Greek, "Valiant for Truth"
against the liberal takeover of the Northern Presbyterian
church and its formerly stalwart Princeton Seminary, and
founder of the Independent Board for Presbyterian Foreign
Missions, of Westminster Seminary, and after being unjustly
suspended from the ministry, of the Orthodox Presbyterian
Church.

That this faithful Christian warrior was also a proponent of
race realism, is proved by two points of evidence. First, in his
book Christianity and Liberalism, he recognizes that the
cause of Christian truth and political liberty are inseparable.
And furthermore, he asserts that egalitarian uniformity is the
enemy of such liberty, and also that the greatest expression of

the principles of political liberty is the particular inheritance of a particular ethnicity:

> The truth is that the materialistic paternalism of the present day, if allowed to go on unchecked, will rapidly make of America one huge "Main Street," where spiritual adventure will be discouraged and democracy will be regarded as consisting in the reduction of all mankind to the proportions of the narrowest and least gifted of the citizens. God grant that there may come a reaction, and that the great principles of Anglo-Saxon liberty may be rediscovered before it is too late!

Second, in his days as a student at Princeton Seminary, he was a proponent of racial segregation. An article discusses this,[49] and on the author's X account[50] we find excerpts from a letter Machen wrote his mother on October 5, 1913:

Timothy Isaiah Cho @tisaiahcho · Sep 2, 2018

"...any time a room is vacant [the colored man] may move over here. If I am to make any objection, now is the time to make it. Of course if he came over here I could simply move out. It would be a big sacrifice to me."

💬 1   🔁 8   ♡ 43   ᴧ   🔖 ⬆

Timothy Isaiah Cho @tisaiahcho · Sep 2, 2018

Explaining why he "most emphatically objects" to the integration of people of color in the dorms, Machen states: "the intimacy of the relation of the men in the same dormitory where there is only one bath-room, exceeds, in some respects, at least, that of table-companionship."

💬 1   🔁 10   ♡ 43   ᴧ   🔖 ⬆

---

49 Timothy Cho, "A Tale of Two Machens," Faithfully Magazine, accessed February 3, 2025, https://faithfullymagazine.com/tale-of-two-machens/.
50 https://x.com/tisaiahcho

Machen goes on to report how in this matter he opposed his beloved professor B. B. Warfield (whom we quoted above praising Dabney):

Timothy Isaiah Cho @tisaiahcho · Sep 2, 2018
"I had a two-hour argument with Warfield on Friday - about as poorly conducted an argument on his side as I ever listened to. My total impression was that, despite his remarkable gifts... he is bitterly lacking in appreciation of the facts of human nature."

It appears from Machen's words that he held to historic Christian race realism, and was willing to defend it, at least in private conversations. Among other things, we would simply note the stark contrast in the fact that leaders in the denomination Machen himself founded now publicly condemn Machen's opinions on this matter.[51]

The final man we'll meet here, and indeed one of the last links in the unbroken chain of centuries of Christian race realism in America, is *Morton H. Smith* (1923–2017), a student at Machen's Westminster Seminary, a Presbyterian minister, and the first Stated Clerk of the Presbyterian Church in America, a Southern church whose founding manifesto, the 1973 "Message to All Churches,"[52] came from Smith's Clerk's office, and self-consciously modeled itself on, and quoted from, Thornwell's 1861 "Address to All Churches" which we considered above. Among other notable accomplishments, Dr. Smith's dissertation, *Studies in*

---

51   See this article for the OPC by D. G. Hart: https://opc.org/os.html?
      article_id=754
52   https://www.pcahistory.org/documents/message.html

Southern Presbyterian Theology,[53] has been a boon to the recovery of knowledge about the faithful men we met above. Dr. Smith also was instrumental in the founding of Reformed Theological Seminary and Greenville Presbyterian Theological Seminary.

Dr. Smith's views on race are presented in an October 1964 article in the *Presbyterian Guardian*.[54] Starting as we did from Paul's statement in Acts 17:26, he speaks of mankind's unity, and his diversity, then moves on to the example of God's segregating Israel from other nations in the Old Testament, stating from God's example, "The principle of segregation as such is not necessarily sinful in and of itself." Considering the New Testament, he draws on the parallel of distinction in sex to prove an important point: "Thus Paul's doctrine of the unity of the church should not be construed as teaching that the church should forget or erase the God-given distinctions. Rather, she should recognize them and develop them in their particular gifts." He goes on to insist that sincere Negro worshipers have been generally welcomed in Southern White churches, and that exceptions had to come only because of the agitation of those visiting merely to press the cause of total integration. In discussing intermarriage, Dr. Smith is more conciliatory than fiery Dr. Dabney, but their agreement is still evident:

---

53 https://www.prpbooks.com/book/studies-in-southern-presbyterian-theology

54 See p125: https://www.opc.org/cfh/guardian/Volume_33/1964-10.pdf

The Bible seems to teach that God has established and thus revealed his will for the human race now to be that of ethnic pluriformity, and thus any scheme of mass integration leading to mass mixing of the races is decidedly unscriptural.

It therefore appears that even in the 1960s, the voice of Christian race realism in American had not been totally silenced.

III: Conclusion

In the testimonies above, we have seen Christian race realism as it was maintained by godly and respected men over at least three hundred years. Historic American Christians have recognized the God-ordained distinctions between races, made efforts to see those distinctions preserved and honored, and when challenged, manfully defended their position, demonstrating that their views were consistent with the highest standards of Christian piety and duty, and that they tended to the temporal and spiritual blessing of every race.

In light of this, we would make a concluding plea. Christians, American or otherwise, need to confess our ignorance of our own history, and endeavor to relearn it. And in so doing, we need to reckon honestly with the fact that Christian race realism is not the strange, novel, or shocking doctrine many say it is. It is certainly not the province of an embarrassing, ungodly fringe of radicals. Rather, for centuries, well into recent history, it was normal and normative in the United States, one of the most Protestant nations in history. It was held by some of the most orthodox Christians, even the most respected Christian ministers, who have ever lived. Moreover, it has been believed and applied most tenaciously in one of the most Christian regions of the entire world, the American South. Contrast this to the fact that the 19th-century racial revolution was led by the likes of William Lloyd Garrison, an anarchist and feminist, and Frederick Douglass, who loved liberal heretics like Strauss and Feuerbach. The 20th-century racial revolution was even more godless, as shown in its patron saint Martin Luther King Jr., an apostate heretic and serial adulterer, who kept close company with communists and Jews. Moreover, the legal monuments to racial egalitarianism also themselves kept evil company: the same court of Chief Justice Earl Warren that ended anti-miscegenation laws in Loving v. Virginia had also ended recitation of prayers and reading of the Bible in public schools in *Engel v. Vitale* and *Abington School District v. Schempp*. The same decade of the victory of "Civil Rights," the 1960s, is still notorious today for its licentiousness and instability. American Christians should not wish to approve of, much less to celebrate, such a low point in their nation's past, and yet they do, in part because of ignorance of history.

With God's help, let us put aside this ignorance. Let us learn from our own fathers in the faith. And let us follow them in speaking truths about race sensibly and scripturally, and in applying those truths in our present evil day with godly prudence.

Chapter 5:
Objections

Having seen the reality of race proven from Scripture and nature, and illustrated from historic Christian thought, we now move on to address objections, which are manifold. We have labored to reduce them to eighteen. To help deal more succinctly, at times we will refer readers to places where a topic has been discussed at greater length, including prior chapters, and our published replies to Charles Johnson, Douglas Wilson, and David Vogel (included as appendices).

Objection 1: Race is not real, except as a social construct

A "social construct" is an artificial category that has reality by convention or societal agreement, and is useful for discussing issues, but has no basis in the reality of the thing it describes. There are various ways race could be called "real," but this objection usually intends to deny that race has a biological reality, that it is rooted in genetics which are passed on in the course of ordinary generation. But the biological reality of race should be obvious. The ancestors of today's Whites, Blacks, and Asians were isolated from each other over the course of many generations, so their genes naturally became isolated. This is a biological reality. They each have distinctive physical features and natural aptitudes that identify them and distinguish them from the others. These are biological realities. Yes, there are less strictly biological things that mark each race, like morality, in their distinctive vices and virtues. But we cannot grant that morality is not at all biological, as least as regards natural proclivities. On the objection that morality and biology have no connection, see chapter 3, under "Morality." Finally, yes there are properly non-biological features that mark races too, like their native languages. But insofar as languages are strongly tied to the people that speak them natively, language still testifies to the reality of race, even if it is not a strict proof of its biological reality. On this topic again see chapter 3. As to the argument from peripheral cases and racial change, see objection 3 below.

Obj. 2: Ethnicity is real, but not race

In common usage of terms, ethnicity is merely a subset of race. They partake of the same reality. See chapters 1 and 3.

Obj. 3: Race is real, but not permanent

We grant that certain features of races can change over time. Usually this happens slowly, and over the long-term. We leave it to God's sovereign freedom that he can change a race more quickly, even miraculously in a moment. But miracles are not the rule of his providence, or of our duty, or of science. If such sudden change should come upon a race, we are committed to empirical honesty, and will adjust our understanding of that race accordingly. Moreover, changes limited to individual persons, families, or even nations, do not disturb the distinctions between races. And large-scale mixing of two races may create a third distinct, real race, but it does not remove the real distinction between the original two unmixed races. See the reply to Wilson.

Obj. 4. Race is real, and permanent, but relatively unimportant

This argument has a generic form, "What does race matter? Better to be colorblind," and a Christian form, "Don't make race an idol. Grace, not race. Major on the majors. Be much in the main things." We address especially the latter. As a warning about relative priority we receive it gladly. We made the same warning ourselves at the end of chapter 1. But this warning is inappropriate when used to ignore the question of the truth of an opinion. And when used to avoid discussing racial issues altogether, it ignores the subtlety of Satan, and closes our eyes to the present reality of his work to destroy even those "main things."

This reality deserves a bit of time to explain. Consider a few analogous things, the first hypothetical. If Satan decided to stir up his servants to start teaching, "2+2=5," and this error became so popular that it started creeping into the church, it would need to be addressed in some manner by the church. This would not mean a math fact is now a "main thing." But if the church allows obvious facts to be overturned openly, reason itself will be overturned, and thus eventually all reasoning from Scripture also. Compare how the Westminster Confession (20.4) says things "contrary to the light of nature...may be lawfully called to account, and proceeded against by the censures of the Church, and by the power of the Civil Magistrate."

A second analogy is not hypothetical, that of feminism. We concede that anti-feminism is not the gospel. But a church that is not anti-feminist will eventually lose the gospel, as history proves. This example is more relevant than most admit: the churches in this age that are the most feminist, are also the most "anti-racist," and the arguments for both errors have striking similarity, e.g. their abuse of Galatians 3:28 (see objection 12 below).

Consider a third analogy from warfare. In its confessions and catechisms the church has strongly fortified and manned the main doctrinal battlements, such as the Trinity, the deity of Christ, and justification by faith alone. And rightly so. But no surprise that Satan would therefore choose to attack the fortress from the rear. And no surprise that he would aid his ambush by convincing watchmen not to sound the alarm, and city elders not to send troops to the back gate, by saying, "This isn't the main gate, it's not worth stirring up such trouble."

This analogy is not idle. Though race realism is not the gospel, Satan is actively using the denial of it to destroy the gospel. The anti-racist Great Replacement he has promulgated would be bad enough if it only opposed the sixth commandment, "Thou shalt not kill." But it is all the worse, and all the more directly a threat to the gospel, because those whom it aims to kill, White men, and among them especially White Anglo-Protestants, are those who have been by far the most responsible for the spread of the gospel. Nearly all the best theologians in nearly all of Christian history have been White, and in the best portions of that history, namely the Reformation and Post-Reformation, they were the Whitest. The best Christian literature has been, and still is today, written and published by White authors. Modern global missions have been, and are today, largely accomplished by White missionaries, which is made possible not only by their unique spiritual heritage, but also by their unique temporal advantages. All should recognize that Christianity and civilization are inseparable, and that the Northwest European sons of Japheth are unique in all the world for their ability to promote both. Among all peoples of the earth, White men have possessed the height of blessings both spiritual and temporal, and they have been most diligent in their use of those blessings for others' good, even and especially their eternal good. No wonder Satan wants to see them ruined. And the denial of race realism is a key to his accomplishment of that ruin.

The denial that race is real brings with it other serious problems. When a race has been convinced it has no particular existence, it naturally loses all incentive to be thankful for its particular blessings, or to serve God particularly according to them. Moreover, among Whites, anti-race-realism teaches them to loathe themselves, not for their sins, but for their very nature, indeed for their historic virtues, which are slandered as great vices. This is a grievous sin against God's law: "Thou shalt love thy neighbor as thyself," and "Honor thy father and thy mother." And though law is distinct from gospel, the gospel does require obedience to the law (John 14:15), and anti-race-realism undermines this obedience. Moreover, it militates against salvation, in that it turns sinners' attention from their real sins, to fake sins invented by modern politicians. When churches make public statements "repenting" of past "racism," they not only slander their fathers, but they also falsely soothe their people's consciences, and thus greatly endanger their souls. For only real repentance from real sins is saving.

Finally we turn the charge back on the objectors. If race is so unimportant, why does the writing of race realists, who are relatively small in number, and have nearly zero power in both church and state, stir up such a firestorm of angry responses, especially from the church? We see the same ministers who say to race realists, "Stop majoring on the minors," go on to pronounce solemn and weighty public condemnations in regard to those "minors." In all honesty, we fear this objection is often not sincere. There are few people in the world or church who actually think racial issues are unimportant, even spiritually.

Obj. 5. Races are real and distinct, but not superior and inferior

We return to the analogy of feminism, which could be described as a denial of "sex realism." Some try a similar compromise against it, which they call "complementarianism," saying that the sexes really differ, and that those differences make them "complementary," while studiously avoiding any implication of the natural inferiority of the female sex, the "weaker vessel" (1 Peter 3:7).

We should not make such compromises. Yes, races are real, and "complementary," as various distinct but interdependent parts of the one body of mankind. But we do not thereby deny that some races are as the head, some as the feet, some more naturally fit for rule, some more naturally fit for submission. We cite the Westminster Larger Catechism's recognition of superiors in gifts (q. 124), and the mutual duties of inferiors and superiors (qq. 125–130). We see no reason to deny that this can be applied to racial differences.

Some would retort, "We agree that wives should obey their husbands, but deny that Blacks should obey Whites." But those statements are not properly parallel. Obedience properly presumes office, as in the former statement: "wives" and "husbands" are offices. But in the second statement, "Blacks" and "Whites" are not offices, but people, standing for whole races. For the first statement to be truly parallel to the second, it would have to say, "Women should obey men." But we deny this statement, as it lacks proper distinctions. We would say rather, "The female sex is inferior to the male sex," and by the proper parallel, "The Black race is inferior to the White race." This inferiority of sex or race, in concrete circumstances, is indeed commonly expressed in inferiority of office: as that of wives to their husbands, so that of Black employees to their White employers, or in the past, of Black slaves to their White masters, or Black subjects to their White colonial rulers. But not always. We recognize that in other concrete circumstances (especially in our egalitarian age) inferiority of sex or race can be present together with superiority of office. For example, a White male employee may have a female or Black boss. In both respects we affirm the fact of inferiority and superiority, and the duties that flow from it.

Another objection comes here, "But I have a highly virtuous, intelligent Black friend, so it's wrong to say the Black race is inferior to the White race." First, not knowing this Black friend ourselves, it is reasonable to question whether the evaluation of his gifts is accurate. In our age of "affirmative action," Whites routinely exaggerate the gifts of non-Whites. Even the left would warn us about the "tokenism" of elevating a minority just because he is a minority. But second, granting the assessment of this friend is true, it is no proof of total racial equality. As races are large populations, we can only speak of racial characteristics by aggregates and averages. There will always be individual exceptions, but these do not disprove sound generalizations. In fact the rarity of the exception is a sound proof the rule is true. A simple reply could be, "Thank the Lord for your friend's gifts. But I have four dozen White friends more virtuous and intelligent than any of the hundreds of Black people I have known. What does this prove?"

Obj. 6. Even if races are inferior, we must show them kindness and compassion

We wholeheartedly affirm the duty of kindness and compassion, especially to inferiors, and we deny the common egalitarian presumption that recognition of one's own superiority necessarily breeds proud, hard-hearted cruelty. Perhaps egalitarians argue this way because they know that if they were given superiority, this is how they would abuse it. If so, this warns us that egalitarians should be kept far from all power and influence.

But we affirm that in virtuous men, and especially virtuous Christian men, a recognition of their own superiority is in fact a powerful motive to kindness and compassion toward their inferiors. Indeed, insofar as a race can know itself to be superior, it thereby is strictly bound to the following duties summarized in the Larger Catechism:

> Q. 129. What is required of superiors towards their inferiors?
>
> A. It is required of superiors, according to that power they receive from God, and that relation wherein they stand, to love, pray for, and bless their inferiors; to instruct, counsel and admonish them; countenancing, commending, and rewarding such as do well; and discountenancing, reproving, and chastising such as do ill; protecting, and providing for them all things necessary for soul and body: and, by grave, wise, holy, and exemplary carriage, to procure glory to God, honor to themselves, and so to preserve that authority which God hath put upon them.

When a superior refuses to do these duties, he is not being kind or compassionate, neither to himself, nor to his inferiors. Rather, he is disobeying God, and failing to serve his fellow men.

We add furthermore that an honest student of history will observe countless instances of White Christians, conscious of their own racial superiority, who have behaved precisely in this upright manner toward their racial inferiors. See the various examples we gave from American history.

Obj. 7. Churches ought never be segregated by race

We deny this, especially because of how revolutionary and harmful it would be if applied consistently. For most churches across the world today are segregated by race *de facto*, and to force a change in this would require an unthinkable imposition of ecclesiastical tyranny.

We also deny that *de jure* racial segregation in the church is always unlawful. We do grant that certain hypothetical forms of racial segregation could be harmful. For example, if a church forbade the mere presence of a single racial stranger in its assemblies. Or if a church in its segregation policies publicly denied the spiritual unity of believers of different races. But we have never seen a single example of either of these hypotheticals, whether in history, or in the present, at least among true Christian churches.

What we have seen in history, however, is some measure of *de jure* racial segregation made according to prudence, in order to prevent real evils. For example, in the 16th century, many Protestants were displaced from their homes by persecution, and in their countries of refuge they usually founded their own separate "Stranger Churches." This is an example of ethnic segregation, but it was quite appropriate, given various practical barriers between the ethnicities, and the various challenges that come to cities from large populations of immigrants.

For another example, in the Southern churches under slavery, Blacks and Whites commonly worshiped in the same church buildings, though Blacks sat in the galleries. This seems to have been a prudent rule, given the vast differences between free Whites and enslaved Africans, and the impropriety of unrestricted social mixing between the two groups. In Old Southern society, such mixing would have been tantamount to violent social revolution, which the church ought never countenance. We would note, however, that the antebellum South featured a much higher degree of racial interaction, even in church, than we usually see in the "integrated" South today. Recall the moving testimonies to this from Rev. E. T. Baird given in chapter 4. So the degree of segregation should not be exaggerated. Or perhaps better said, we should recognized that the strong class segregation that slavery already imposed at that time, meant that further geographical, domestic, and ecclesiastical segregation of the races was not necessary.

All through the ensuing strife of war, and Reconstruction, and "civil rights," until fairly recently, Southern churches still maintained some racial segregation, whether in segregated seating, segregated congregations, or segregated denominations. The liberal Southern Presbyterian church the present author grew up in had distinctly White and Black churches that were united in one presbytery. Now we cannot say, not knowing each church's particular situation, that every policy in every church was perfectly prudent and just. But neither can we grant that every policy that segregates at all by race is *ipso facto* evil. Especially when we consider how the century spanning from the 1860s to the 1960s was full of racial strife, which at times overflowed into deadly violence. If an objector could not grant racial segregation on other grounds, could he not at least grant it on the grounds of preventing racial violence from spilling over into the church, and thereby disrupting its worship and service?

To deal with this question a bit more abstractly, we should not deny to the visible church the authority, and indeed the duty, to order outward circumstances, to maintain its membership, and determine its policies, in a way that best conduces for the good of its own people under Christ. That the visible church must so order outward circumstances, is demanded by the fact that it exists in this present world, and must therefore deal with temporal realities, from the reality of mowing its lawn and repairing its building, to the more weighty reality of racial difference. That the visible church has a right to order such circumstances, is proven by the Jerusalem council in Acts 15. In it, during a time of strife between Jews and Gentiles, the church determined to require the Gentiles, among other things, to restrain their own liberty in eating certain foods (vv. 20, 29), in order not to be a scandal to the Jews. Situations differ, but the principle remains: the church may, and must, deal wisely with the circumstances of this life in which it finds itself.

Consider an analogous concrete example. Churches today usually practice strict segregation in their seating, as members are separated by their families. Rarely would a policy ever have to be made to enforce this, but in the strange case that children, or especially spouses, were routinely mixing with other families, imposing such a policy might be prudent to avoid scandal. Whether imposed by rule or not, is such segregation in seating a sin? Of course not. Neither therefore is it by analogy a sin, at least not in itself, for the auditorium to be segregated by race. For like family, race is a merely natural distinction; indeed, races are highly extended families.

Consider the analogy of segregation by language. The madness of modern immigration has brought Babel to our cities. Some places seem to be becoming multi-lingual overnight. What do we do when a sincere seeker or convert wants to come to church with us, but does not speak English well enough to profit from the sermons? Some churches offer translation services, or English classes. Others do their best to help the visitor find a church nearby that worships in his native tongue. In many cases, the best choice will be to tell the immigrant, with love, that it is best for his own interests, as well as those of his host country, for him to return to his own land, and find (or help to found) the best church that he can among his people. Whatever the solution, some type of segregation is required. Those who may be totally united in the Lord, because they are not united in one natural respect, language, cannot be totally united in the outward communion of the visible church. It is no sin to recognize this is the case with language, and to deal accordingly. We challenge any objector to argue why these same distinctions cannot be applied to segregation by race. Especially as in the concrete, ethnic and linguistic differences so often come together. On this see chapter 3.

Consider also the analogy of distinct national churches, e.g. the Presbyterian Church of East Africa (in Kenya), versus the Presbyterian Church in America. When churches are segregated in this manner, we understand that segregation is no sin, but again, a prudent ordering of outward circumstances. This happens even when the national boundaries between the churches are relatively small, as when churches planted in White Canada by White Americans are eventually divided off into their own Canadian denomination. Such separation is no proof of spiritual disunity, but rather serves spiritual unity, by equipping the churches for freer gospel witness to their own people, and to the world. What then when even stronger national boundaries are observed to exist within the confines of one place? Is separation therefore not allowed, because the distinct nations happen to reside in the same region? We recognize this analogy is complicated by questions of distance, finances, politics, and history. But one thing it certainly proves, is that ecclesiastical segregation on the basis of national distinctions, is not in itself a sin, but may in fact be prudent in the proper circumstances.

We have not even mentioned the positive benefits that recommend ethnic homogeneity in church. Diversity brings difficulty, but similarity is a help to unity in every sphere, even the ecclesiastical. The example of Dutch immigrant churches established in the 20th century in North America powerfully illustrates this fact. Though not unwelcoming to the non-Dutch, these churches are largely ethnically homogeneous. They thus partake of the ethnic character of their members: like Dutch businesses and homes, Dutch churches are well-organized, well-funded, and highly successful. The Dutch culture of strong families, hard work, and stubborn virtue suffuses everything in church. For example, it is not uncommon to see three or four generations sitting together in the pew. Nor is it rare for a church to have hundreds of committed members who never miss a service, and among them, a greater number of qualified men than it ever strictly needs to serve in eldership. Nor are Dutch elders slack in duty, but are proverbially diligent in visiting, teaching, and serving in their consistories, classes, and synods.

These blessings are not merely ethnic. They are most certainly also spiritual. But we cannot deny that Dutch spiritual blessings come in part by the help of Dutch ethnic blessings. Nor can we deny that if their Dutch ethnicity was diluted or replaced, even if all other things remained the same, it is unlikely that those churches would enjoy such degree of blessing. Many non-Dutch churches, even those which we believe to be more pure in worship and doctrine, nonetheless have never experienced the same sort and degree of blessings as the Dutch, we believe in part because they do not benefit from Dutch ethnic homogeneity. We leave to various churches, Dutch or otherwise, how to apply this observation in their own circumstances.

Finally, we plead the example of various non-White racially-homogenous churches today, for whom the right to racial separation is sometimes asserted, even publicly,[55] without much opposition. We suspect because of this that at least some of the animus against racial segregation in White churches is more properly called anti-White, than anti-segregation.

---

55 E.g. see here: https://sola.network/article/why-ethnic-specific-churches-still-important-interview/

Obj. 8. Paul rebuked Peter for racial segregation in Galatians 2:11-14

This objection fails to distinguish properly. Peter, a Jew, did "separate himself" from eating with the Gentiles (v. 12). We could call this a sort of racial segregation, formally. But the problem is not with the form, but with the reason. Paul rebukes Peter's actions as a failure to walk uprightly according to the truth of the gospel (v. 14). How did Peter deny the gospel by his actions? The context is the conflict with the Judaizing heretics, against whom Galatians is chiefly written. It appears certain of these heretics were the men who came "from James," who caused Peter to withdraw from the Gentiles (v. 12). Their opposition to fellowship with Gentiles was not simply racial, it was chiefly religious. They believed that circumcision (a religious sign, only incidentally racial) was still required, not only by God's command, as an abiding sacrament (as with baptism in the New Testament), but in particular, required for justification, as a meritorious work. Therefore Peter's yielding to their shunning of the Gentiles was in principle a denial of justification by faith alone. Moreover, it was a hypocritical denial of Peter's own prior practice: before the heretics swayed him, he ate with Gentiles (v. 12), and lived like them (v. 14). It appears from Paul's argument that Peter's initial practice was a statement, not of racial egalitarianism, but of spiritual communion (just as the sharing of possessions in Acts 2:45 does not teach communism, but brotherly Christian love). By that practice Peter had clearly communicated, with apostolic authority, that the believing Gentiles belonged to Christ by faith just as much as did the believing Jews. His cowardly change of practice then sharply contradicted this. Note furthermore how Paul argues in verse 16, powerfully insisting that justification is not by works of the law, but by faith in Jesus Christ, and how this passage serves as a transition to Paul's further treatment of justification in the ensuing chapters.

What is condemned here, then, is the denial of the gospel of justification by faith alone, not racial segregation in itself. Paul's rebuke left Peter free to practice racial segregation in other ways that did not implicate him in heresy. No doubt simply by being Jewish, he ate much more often with his Jewish family, and with other fellow Jews. No doubt when he did eat with Gentiles, he would take care to do so in a way that did not scandalize his fellow Jews, especially in that unique time of transition, in which it was still permissible, though no longer obligatory, to keep the ceremonial law. Compare William Perkins on this passage: "The fact of Peter considered by itself, is not a sin: for Paul did the like in playing the Jew: but the circumstances make it a sin."[56]

Nor should we speculate that Peter's prior eating with Gentiles proves that members of the apostolic church practiced totally promiscuous social fellowship between all races, whether between Jews and Gentiles, or among various Gentile nations. We assume that in the distinct local churches of that time, just as today, their ethnic character would normally reflect that of their neighborhood. Compare how

---

56 William Perkins, *A Commentarie or Exposition, Upon the Five First Chapters of the Epistle to the Galatians,* John Legat, 1604, p. 107.
https://quod.lib.umich.edu/e/eebo/A09383.0001.001/1:6?rgn=div1;view=fulltext

Acts 6:1 alludes in the church to distinct parties, "Grecians" and "Hebrews," and Colossians 3:11 to "Barbarian" and "Scythian." Whatever the case was in the early church, this passage does not condemn the racial segregation practiced in the historic churches of the American South, as this was a prudent application of church power in their particular circumstances, and did not implicate them in any denial of justification by faith, or of the spiritual unity there is in Christ between believers of different races. Nor did it even remove all social interaction between the races, but rather set up prudent boundaries so that their interaction would not bring harm and scandal.

Obj. 9. Inter-racial marriages are legitimate

We dealt at length with this objection in the reply to Johnson, argument 15. We quote most of that portion here:

> I do not assert that inter-ethnic or inter-racial marriage is in itself unlawful, strictly forbidden in all its forms by Scripture and nature, as in the case of so-called "gay marriage." I did and do affirm there are examples of it in Scripture, and though examples do not themselves make law, I do not assert that they are all bad examples. What I do assert is this, that given various serious factors—the enormous importance of the choice of one's spouse, the weighty consequences that choice brings for the couple, their children, their family, and their nation, the blessings that come from affinity and similarity in marriage, the special love we owe to family, kin, and nation, the differences God has established in providence between races and nations, the woeful reality of racial strife, which appears only to be

increasing, and other not insignificant special challenges that come to spouses and their children through inter-racial marriage—it is usually not wise, not prudent, not best to marry across a large ethnic boundary, and all the less so the greater that boundary is. And yes, we do affirm, as should all people, that it is a sin not to be wise, not to be prudent, and not to choose the best we can, even among things that may be lawful in themselves.

To address Mr. Johnson's concern directly: I do not assert that what is unlawful is inter-racial marriage per se. Rather, what is unlawful is to be imprudent. And inter-racial marriage is often imprudent. Indeed in some extreme forms it is always imprudent, or at least so often imprudent that rules should be enforced against it, in the family, or even in the state, as in Christian America until 1967.

It appears to us this is the chief practical objection on the minds of Christian opponents of race realism, so we will take a bit more space here to deal with two particular arguments they often bring.

(1) *Marriage is a matter of free choice. Christians may marry any Christian (1 Cor. 7:39).*

It is true that marriage is a matter of "free choice," if by that term is meant, the uncoerced consent of the will of an adult capable of giving it. Both spouses must freely say, "I do." Even in the case of an arranged marriage, this freedom must be honored (so it was in Rebekah's case, Gen. 24:57–58). But this is not all that is meant here. For prohibiting inter-racial marriage does not coerce anyone's consent. It simply forbids the granting of that consent in certain discrete cases. "Free choice" in this objection speaks not of a natural freedom in giving consent without coercion, according to the nature of the marriage vow, but of a libertarian freedom in doing anything, without influence or opposition, according to a person's whim. It is commonly expressed in the phrase, "I'll do whatever I want." But if what you want is immoral, or imprudent, or harmful, you shouldn't do it, and you may, and in many cases must, be forbidden from doing it, by the exercise of a legitimate authority.

The apostle Paul is exercising such an authority in 1 Corinthians 7:39. He says the Christian widow may not marry anyone she wants, without qualification. She may marry "only in the Lord." The prudence of this counsel is explained at greater length in 2 Corinthians 6:14, "Be not unequally yoked together with unbelievers: for what fellowship hath righteousness with unrighteousness? and what communion hath light with darkness?"

Paul's command to exercise prudence in regard to religious differences recommends a similar exercise of prudence when it comes to non-religious differences. We ought not enter marriage "unequally yoked" in other ways as well. The question of Amos 3:3 is relevant even in natural things, "Can two walk together, except they be agreed?" This is recognized by common wisdom, that a good marriage demands compatibility. *Similis simili gaudet*, like rejoices in like. Not all differences will make a marriage choice imprudent, but the larger the difference, the more likely it will be a barrier to domestic happiness.

Consider other differences that are not religious, but that would render a marriage inadvisable. What if the man is fifty years older than the woman? Or the woman twenty years older than the man? What if the man is significantly less intelligent than the woman? What if the man and woman do not speak a common language? "Only in the Lord" does not allow us to ignore these natural differences. Nor does it allow us to ignore natural differences of race, and all the other differences that usually come with it. See chapter 3.

(2) *Opposing inter-racial marriage calls into question legitimate marriages, and thus threatens discontentment.*

An imprudent marriage is not thereby illegitimate. Except in cases where previously established civil statutes declare it to be invalid (as in Ezra 10), an inter-racial marriage between one man and one woman, established publicly by free consent, is valid, and permanently binding. "What therefore God hath joined together, let not man put asunder" (Matt. 19:6).

Nor does a later recognition of an imprudent choice of spouse require discontentment. It may bring shame and disappointment, but this should be dealt with by confession before God, commitment to act with greater prudence in the future, and cheerful service in the present circumstances. God is very merciful and gracious, and will deal tenderly with those who humbly recognize they've made mistakes.

This is a principle that applies beyond the present controversy. People often choose spouses imprudently, even within their race. I have met long-married Christian couples who freely say that knowing what they both know now, they should have never married, but that God has over-ruled their youthful foolishness and blessed them far beyond all expectations. We see no reason why an inter-racial couple could not humbly recognize their marriage was imprudent, while gladly submitting to God's perfect providence, and committing to serve each other, until death do them part.

Obj. 10. Ethnically-specific laws in the Old Testament were unique to ancient Israel

The Mosaic civil law did require ethnic discrimination in various ways, including in its strict prohibition of Israelite-Canaanite marriage. For more examples see chapter 2. The ancient commonwealth of Israel no longer exists, and therefore this law that was its constitution has expired. However, that law's general equity, the universal moral principles on which it was based, could not and did not expire. As long as there remain moral grounds for ethnic discrimination, then such discrimination may and ought to be practiced, and even codified in modern law. We must always respect the difference in times and circumstances between our nations and ancient Israel. But to draw on the Mosaic law for examples and guidance in writing our own laws, is both prudent, and reverent, as there is no other civil constitution in the history of mankind that was given by divine inspiration. None of its laws, even its ethnically-specific laws, were in the least unjust. Nor therefore would similar laws in similar circumstances today be unjust.

Some will argue here that Old Testament law was typical, speaking of Christ, salvation, and the New Testament to come. We do not deny such spiritual interpretation of Old Testament law. But we do deny that therefore we may make no political and social interpretation of it, as we did in chapter 2. Such interpretation is common in sound Christian authors throughout history, and we are not ashamed to follow them in this. See the reply to Johnson, argument 11.

Obj. 11. Old Testament racial segregation was only on account of morality and religion

It is true that the racial segregation enjoined in the civil law had moral and religious reasons. God says Canaanite daughters were not to be taken in marriage, "For they will turn away thy son from following me, that they may serve other gods" (Deut. 7:3). But are morality and religion therefore the only reasons? Was there no other ground of equity in such laws, whether from natural affection and affinity, or some other principles observed by prudence and propriety? If so, this must be proven, not merely asserted.

Moreover, if it is proven, it is no argument against wise policies of racial segregation today. For even if those segregation laws had no other reason than morality and religion, this does nothing to hinder our own segregation laws from citing other equitable reasons. Promoting the morality and religion of a people may be the highest aim of government, but it is not its only aim.

Yet whatever other reasons may recommend segregation today, the most compelling reason for it is precisely that given by God in Deuteronomy, that of morality and religion. Historic Southern segregation protected a more virtuous, civilized, and Christianized White population from harmful association with Blacks who were significantly less virtuous, civilized, and Christianized. Recall from chapter 3 that Blacks committed 64% of U.S. murders in 2021, and Black men are four times more likely to be incarcerated than White men, even after statistics are adjusted for income. Black families are proverbially broken and dysfunctional. Black Christianity often has more emotion than substance. The most sound, orthodox, historic Protestant churches in our nation were founded, and today are led, almost entirely by Whites. The rare Black ministers among them are often notoriously subversive (we gave a few examples in chapter 1). Neither are there similarly orthodox Black churches, nor do Black people join solid White churches, in any significant number. We believe and hope the grace of Christ will change this one day, but at present, it is an undeniable reality.

We do not attribute to all Black people the same form and depth of godless degeneracy as marked the ancient Canaanites. But the analogy does hold, as does the equity of putting up some legal barriers today for the protection of our White Christian people. If someone should object that Whites are far less Christian than they used to be, we do affirm this with deep sadness. But Blacks are far less Christian than they used to be as well, and we would not affirm that their own course of apostasy has been any slower than that of Whites. Moreover, the spiritual regression of our own people should give us all the more, not less, a reason to impose laws to protect them from further spiritual harm.

Some argue from evangelism here, that segregation would keep non-White souls from hearing the gospel. They apply the same argument to immigration: let the heathen freely come to our shores, and bring the mission field to us! Better reasoning would say that just as with ancient Israel, so America will be all the more a light to the nations as its own spiritual character is carefully protected from harmful foreign influence. Also, history casts strong doubt upon this argument. The most famous and fruitful 19th-century foreign missionaries were sent from White nations, in a time in which those nations' racial homogeneity was more carefully protected by law. Moreover, the antebellum Southern Presbyterians were more successful in evangelizing Blacks than our White churches under integration. We challenge readers to consider the work of John L. Girardeau[57] and C. C. Jones,[58] then to supply even one example of an evangelist among our modern "anti-racists" who has been so highly beloved among Blacks, and so beneficial to their everlasting souls.

On this objection, see also the reply to Johnson, argument 14.

Obj. 12. There is neither Jew nor Greek in Christ, Galatians 3:28

This passage, and its parallel in Colossians 3:11, is treated as an invincible "defeater" argument against race realism. Yet it is not. Rather, it reveals the false, unbiblical, egalitarian presumptions of those who think it is. This is so by three clear reasons.

---

57   Sally Davey, "John L. Girardeau: Minister to the Slaves of South Carolina," *Banner of Truth*, February 11, 2015.
      https://banneroftruth.org/us/resources/articles/2015/john-l-girardeau-minister-to-the-slaves-of-south-carolina/

58   Charles C. Jones, *The Religious Instruction of the Negroes in the United States*, Thomas Purse, 1842.

First, relatively few men are "in Christ." The majority of the globe does not even profess Christianity. And among those called into the communion of the visible church, the Lord Jesus himself says, "few are chosen" (Matt. 22:14). We gladly affirm the spiritual unity of all men who believe in Christ, from every nation, tribe, and tongue. They have "one Lord, one faith, one baptism, one God and Father of all" (Eph. 4:5–6). But of the rest we say, they are "strangers from the covenants of promise, having no hope, and without God in the world" (Eph. 2:12). We doubt that our opponents really wish to say that their proposed egalitarian political equality should apply only to true believing Christians. This would require magistrates to search men's souls, and see the secrets of their hearts, before they granted them citizenship in their utopian non-segregated commonwealth. They neither can do this, nor should.

Second, if some would take "in Christ" to speak, not of individual faith, but of the economy of the covenant of grace, by way of contrast with the Old Testament when Christ had not yet come in the flesh, this also makes no sense. For Galatians 3:28 was true in the Old Testament as well. Abraham and his faithful believing servant, Eliezer of Damascus (Gen. 15:2; ch. 24), both believed in Christ, and enjoyed spiritual unity, despite their ethnic, domestic, and political inequality (see esp. Gen. 24:27). Some similarly cite Ephesians 2:12–14 against race realism, as if the coming of the New Testament had overturned all ethnic distinctions. We agree that Christ's coming revoked the civil law of Moses, and the ceremonial law, and inaugurated the evangelism of the entire globe (Matt. 28:19). But in the Great Commission, "teach all nations" assumes that nations are distinct, and will remain so, even as they will in heaven (Rev. 7:19).

Third, suppose we granted (though we don't concede it) that Paul's words required a "race-blind" society, in which ethnic distinctions like "Jew" and "Greek" were totally ignored, or even intentionally erased, by the promotion of miscegenation. We would then by force of argument have to grant that the other distinctions in the verse should also be ignored. Society would have to be, not only race-blind, but also class-blind, and sex-blind. Together with slavery, all political or economic subjection would have to be abolished, because "there is neither bond nor free." The recent laws that countenance "gay marriage" would have to stand, and we could not say anything against feminism, or even transgenderism, because "there is neither male nor female." We expect every true Christian to recoil at the absurdity of these conclusions. But we are not unaware that certain liberal heretics boldly assert all these absurdities from this same text. Christians have no business joining them in such a shameless twisting of the Scriptures.

Obj. 13. Racial minorities deserve civil rights

We distinguish: civil rights are not natural rights. The former are positive, changeable according to circumstances, and the latter moral, permanent, and unchangeable. Moreover, natural rights are determined according to nature, and not all men are entirely the same by nature. Equality before the law does not mean equality of nature, or of status. Nor does it require an equality of privileges, especially if such equality is enforced in a way that destroys or ignores natural distinctions. Finally, civil rights are good only as they tend toward the securing of civil common good.

So to be specific, no man has a natural right to vote, to hold civil office, or to live in whatever neighborhood, or make use of whatever water fountain, amusement park, or classroom he may choose. These are all privileges, and it is no sin in itself not to grant them to any particular group, especially when the group is an unassimilated foreign racial minority. Now, a civil right to these things may be granted, even to foreign minorities, but this should only be done in a way that best serves the common good. Moreover, even after such a civil right is granted, it can be revoked without any sin against natural or moral law, and should be, when it becomes obvious that it has failed to serve the common good.

The question of civil rights for racial minorities, then, is, "Do they serve the common good?" Let's consider some specifics. Did Black suffrage serve the common good? Not in the least: Blacks consistently vote for the worst politicians, as do other racial minorities in America. Did it serve the common good to forbid racial discrimination in housing? It did not: rather, it spurred "White flight," a form of ethnic replacement in which White families have to abandon their homes, some of them various times over, out of legitimate fear for their safety, when non-Whites move into their area in any significant number. Did it serve the common good to integrate White schools at gunpoint? No, it did not. The influence of Blacks upon the morality and safety of White children has not been wholesome, to put it lightly. The presence of distinct Black and White intelligence in the same classroom now means neither group can be well served according to its needs. And the particular "White flight" that school integration caused, in the fairly recent founding of the nation's many private schools, and in the more recent trend toward home-schooling, has drained public schools of their best and most devoted families, quickening their downward spiral into the moral and intellectual abyss. We are not blaming Whites for the condition of the public schools: we affirm the wisdom of not using them. But as the majority of our nation's children still use them, their degradation means the degradation of our nation.

We could go on, but we conclude in general that we find the "civil rights" narrative of bold sit-ins at lunch counters to be a sentimental cover-up for what was in fact a destructive social revolution, which has brought serious harm to the majority White population in America, as well as to Blacks and other minorities. Such civil rights deserve to be repealed.

Obj. 14. Discrimination, partiality, and prejudice are sins

These things are not sins in themselves, but only in their abuse. Morality must honor particularity, and in that respect it can be immoral not to discriminate. For example, when obeying "Honor thy father and thy mother," it is essential to discriminate my father and my mother from all others. It is true that Scripture condemns partiality under the term "respect of persons" (James 2:1, 9), but this is properly defined as the making of a judgment according to qualities of persons which do not support that judgment. In the context of James 2, the example is that of giving a rich man special honor in the church, though wealth is not a reliable indicator of a good spiritual condition. In the same passage, James reminds his hearers that the wealthy are persecutors of poor Christians, and blasphemers (vv. 6–7). This reminder could be described as a wholesome apostolic prejudice, made according to reasonable generalization from experience. So however strongly James condemns partiality (rightly defined), he does not condemn all prejudice.

When applied to racial matters, discrimination and prejudice can be not only wholesome, but even life-saving. When a White father observes a dozen dark young men arriving at a gas station, it is no sin for him to stop the pump and leave immediately. When a White woman finds herself alone in an elevator (not recommended), and a tall, strong Black man walks in, she does no wrong to him to exit quickly. When a White family sees neighboring houses begin to be filled up with unfriendly foreigners, we cannot blame them for at least considering a move. To teach Whites to be ashamed of such prudent self-preservation shows a great lack of love for them, and a suppression, whether ignorant or malicious, of facts observed by common sense.

Obj. 15. Racial hatred, animosity, and vainglory are sins

Yes they are, and we by no means advocate them. Furthermore, in speaking of the sins of other races, we do not forget the besetting sins of White men, or of the degeneracy found in our own race. Moreover, insofar as Whites have greater power, they have greater responsibility, and their sins are also all the more destructive. The 20th century in Europe revealed the horrors that can come from the abuse of White political and military power. And insofar as Whites have spiritual blessings above other races, God will hold them all the more strictly to account for those blessings, as well as for their unthankful rejection of them.

We deny, however, that a reasonable assertion of racial superiority, even in regard to one's own race, is necessarily hateful or vainglorious. On this see objection 6 above.

Obj. 16. We ought not play racial identity politics, or adopt a victim mentality

We sympathize with this objection. We find so-called "critical race theorists" to be shrill racial partisans, and believe all men have a duty to flee unthinking bigotry and cultivate a liberal mind. We furthermore abhor a spirit of ungrateful complaining, even under real oppression, and especially an envious critique of others for their privileges, whether deserved or undeserved.

We do not deny that White men ought to cultivate racial solidarity, and protest the persecution of their race. This is an urgent need, and without it, Whites will not survive. But they should do it always from a position of confident superiority, and of calm, sober resolve. Moreover, they must do it with deep humility and meekness, and with sincere repentance, recognizing that their racial birthright is a gift from God, which he could justly take from them, if they should not repent of their own sins, or if in prosecuting their just cause they should mimic their wicked enemies, by asserting their rights in manner that is proud, ungrateful, envious, rebellious, or inhumane. Compare objection 6 above.

Obj. 17. Speaking so bluntly about a race's sins will drive that race away from the gospel

We grieve to hear Christians argue this way, for the truth is the exact opposite. Christ said, "They that are whole need not a physician; but they that are sick" (Luke 5:31). No man will seek the remedy before he knows his own disease. And how will he know, if no one tells him?

In the New Testament, the apostles and evangelists converted thousands from various races, yet they by no means withheld racially-specific condemnations of sin. Stephen in Acts 7 spoke freely of Jewish sins. As did Peter preaching at Pentecost, when three thousand "men of Israel" (Acts 2:22) were "pricked in their heart" after he condemned them for crucifying the Lord (vv. 36–37). Paul, the apostle to the Gentiles, pronounces specific condemnations upon specific Gentile nations. He chides the Greeks for their absurd multiplication of false gods (Acts 17:22–23, cf. v. 16), and how their vaunted wisdom kept them from submitting to the "foolishness" of Christ crucified (1 Cor. 1:22–23). And most notably, he says to Titus of the Cretians, "One of themselves, even a prophet of their own, said, The Cretians are alway liars, evil beasts, slow bellies. This witness is true." (Titus 1:12–13). We cannot think of many racial slurs today that are more intrinsically derogatory than "evil beasts." Yet Paul makes no qualifications: it is always so, and this witness is true. And not only that, but the knowledge and application of this truth is necessary for the Cretians to be saved: "Wherefore rebuke them sharply, that they may be sound in the faith" (v. 13).

Clearly implied is that even men from degenerate races may become "sound in the faith." But this will never happen without their confessing and forsaking that degeneracy. Moreover, even if and when by grace a man does rise above his race, his natural connection to his kin will bring constant temptation to regress. Christ warns in Luke 14:26, "If any man come to me, and hate not his father, and mother, and wife, and children, and brethren, and sisters, yea, and his own life also, he cannot be my disciple." We ought not spare men of any race from similar wholesome warnings.

Some argue here from the doctrine of total depravity, as if all men were exactly equal in their sins, citing Paul, "They are all gone out of the way, they are together become unprofitable; there is none that doeth good, no, not one." (Rom. 3:12). But properly that doctrine teaches that sin has rendered every man by nature incapable of doing any spiritual good, spiritually, unto salvation (Heb. 11:6; cf. 1 Cor. 2:14). It does not deny that sinful men can and do exercise natural virtue, that some men notably exercise it more than others, or that certain groups of sinners are more deeply vicious than the rest. By nature, all men are depraved, but not all men are degenerate.

Finally, this objection is often made with unstated exceptions. Many of the same preachers who would never mention Black murder or fornication from the pulpit have no trouble multiplying public condemnations of the besetting sins, real or alleged, of Whites. This is but one example of how "anti-racists" should rather be called "anti-White."

Obj. 18. Speaking about these matters is divisive, destroying precious unity, especially in the church

We wish with all our heart this issue did not occasion such division as it does. It seems that any assertion of race realism today, no matter how calm and charitable, stirs up vitriolic anger, and a consequent disturbance of peace and unity, especially in church. But we must ask two questions here. First, whose fault is this? It was not Elijah that troubled Israel (1 Kings 18:17–18). And second, though unity is very precious, at what cost must it be purchased? If in order to gain unity we must suppress common-sense truths about racial differences, censure White men for speaking for their people, and impose silence about White genocide and suicide, then the cost of unity is far too high.

We believe there is a better way. Indeed, it is the only safe way to arrive at unity and peace. It is the way of the apostle Paul: "By manifestation of the truth commending ourselves to every man's conscience in the sight of God" (2 Cor. 4:2). This is our aim, and by God's grace, we will continue in it.

Chapter 6:
Application

Having introduced and defined Christian race realism, demonstrated it from Scripture and nature, illustrated it from history, and addressed objections to it, we now endeavor to apply it. As we said in chapter 1,

We must name, praise, and protect racial distinctions. As in all other matters, we must think and live according to reality. The application will of course stir up the greatest opposition, but truth not practiced might as well not be taught. If race is real, real duties follow.

We will consider these duties under nine headings, of which the last two, politics and church, will receive the most attention.

1. Study

The first duty regards our mind, that we must remedy our ignorance on racial matters.

In specific, reading up on current events regarding race is important for seeing the urgency of the issue. The "Great

Replacement" of Whites in their own countries is often denied as a false conspiracy theory, but the evidence for it is obvious to anyone willing to see it. Compare the first part of chapter 1.

Reading history also will help many to see that much of what is dismissed as "racist" today used to be simple common sense, and that the "progressive" narrative privileges novel views that are the product of destructive, anti-Christian social revolutions. Consider our dealing with history in chapter 4.

Reading biology and social science will help to give good grounding in empirical reality, and to dissolve false idealistic egalitarian assumptions. The data on criminality and on intelligence by race, when soberly considered, are particularly enlightening. See chapter 3. But we would emphasize as we did there that statistics should never replace common sense. Rather, formal science trains us for the better exercise of informal science, in our daily recognition of reality.

Reading Scripture is of utmost importance, because it explains the only way of salvation, without which all our knowledge will profit us nothing, but also because on this issue of race it offers much wisdom, and all of it divine. As we saw in chapter 2, the Bible teaches that God himself established racial difference, and recognized and protected that difference in various ways, including in the civil law of Moses. Moreover, Christians need to know the Bible well to counter the manifold abuses of it by the "anti-racists," some of which we addressed directly in chapter 5.

2. Defense

Those who by careful study have been convinced of race realism have the duty to defend it, according to their calling and ability. This requires both courage and prudence, especially in our present "cancel culture." In this defense, two specific difficulties are worth considering.

First, opponents label the race realist with various terms of reproach, including *racist, White nationalist, White supremacist,* and in the church, *kinist.* The best way to respond to this is first by discerning what those terms actually signify. Asking, "What do you mean?" can reveal the person has not thought through the relevant matters, or that he's simply interested in destruction, not discussion. If so, it may be prudent just to end the conversation, perhaps with a rebuke. But if the person is willing, asking such a question can open a productive conversation. It may offer an opportunity to put the term to a good use by agreeing on a wholesome definition. For example, "If racist only means I think that race is real, and have a special love and loyalty for my own race, without malice toward any other, then I'm not ashamed to be a racist." Or, "Of course I'm a White nationalist: my own nation is White, I love it, and I'm eager for its blessing and preservation." Or, "Everyone is a White supremacist of some sort. Even leftists recognize that White nations presently rule supreme over the world. The difference is, they hate it, and I think it is a kind gift of God's providence."

My judgment is that race realists under pressure are too quick to totally reject such terms. This brings harm to the cause because it opens them to the charge of striving about words (2 Tim. 2:14; 1 Tim. 6:4), by focusing on terms more than on substance. It also indirectly affirms the reproachful use of terms which could serve as positive descriptions, and fails to defend like-minded men who have embraced them as such. Thus in an effort to be strategic, it threatens defeat by shooting allies, and not joining them in a united front against a common enemy. This can be illustrated with the term "kinist." I myself prefer to be called a "race realist," but I accept the term "kinist" because my disagreements with those who prefer that term are not essential to race realism, or they are relatively small, especially when contrasted with the errors of our common opponents. For example, as regards the overture on kinism presented to the 2019 synod of the Christian Reformed Church,[59] I stand against the CRC's egalitarian abuse of Scripture, and with nearly all the "Commonly Held Beliefs of Kinists" (listed on p. 503).

Of course there will always be intramural debates among Christian race realists. But this is no reason to "cancel" each other. If we lament that racial egalitarians uncharitably denounce us, it is hypocritical to turn and do the same to each other. Moreover, some Christian race realists can be odd, unsavory, or even in some respects ungodly. In that case we ought to oppose precisely what is wrong, while still celebrating what is right. We need not fear the common tactic of "guilt by association." Indeed, if it were applied with equity, the professing Christian racial egalitarians would be more guilty by far, for their opinion on race is the same as

---

59 Christian Reformed Church, *Agenda for Synod 2019*, Christian Reformed Church in North America, 2019, p. 489.

that embraced by the majority of the most godless anti-Christians of our present evil age, and the worst liberal and moderate subversives in the church itself.

Second, defending these matters among Christian brethren calls for special care. When speaking privately, we ought to recognize where people are, and where they're not, and be careful not to force them to come farther than they're willing (cf. 1 Cor. 3:2). We will be helped in patience by remembering our own prior struggles coming to the truth on race, and the high social cost of standing up for it, recognizing that to embrace the truth and pay that cost will take rare fortitude. As well as patience, this calls for humble prayer, that God would open eyes and strengthen feeble knees.

Opposition from Christians will be harder than from the world, as of all men, we love fellow believers most (Ps. 16:3), and Christian unity is such a precious gift (Ps. 133:1). It will be hardest of all when opposition comes from church elders, especially when joined by the threat of censure. If false charges do come, we counsel not yielding one inch on the truth, but also bearing the process patiently, giving honor to the established order of Christ's church, not forgetting to esteem church leaders very highly in love for their work's sake (1 Thess. 5:13), even if this aspect of their work is being wrongly done. If the time comes to leave a church, make sure to leave with a good conscience, preserving peace as far as in you lies (Rom. 12:18). And then make sure to find another faithful church as soon as possible. Satan would love to ruin bold defenders of the truth, by cutting them off totally from the "church of the living God, the pillar and ground of the truth" (1 Tim. 3:15). More on this under point 9 below.

We conclude with the all-important grace of charity, which is so sadly rare in controversies on these matters. Whenever race is discussed, we ought to be ashamed to hear how quickly Christian conversation degenerates to bold denunciations, critique of error to condemnations of heresy, and concern for souls to declarations of hypocrisy. Paul warns that if I have not charity, I am nothing (1 Cor. 13:2), and shows by his example that we ought to spend ourselves in love even for those who hate us for our love (2 Cor. 12:15). The very truth of race realism would call us to this. For if we ought to exercise the natural virtue of love for kin, how much more ought we to exercise the supernatural virtue of Christian charity, which shows its excellence over mere natural affection, by extending itself even to our enemies (Matt. 5:44).

3. Repentance

The truths we have presented thus far cut deep. They call for the total destruction of the idol of egalitarianism, which is one of the most prominent false gods among the modern pantheon, widely worshiped even in professing Christian churches, especially in the form of "anti-racism." Therefore we cannot be faithful to this cause without calling for deep, serious repentance. We will speak politically and ecclesiastically below: here we speak personally. Reader, you must repent of denying that race is real. You must repent of persecuting others for saying race is real, and for living accordingly. You must repent of envy, of covetous discontentment with the fact that men of certain races enjoy blessings those of other races don't enjoy in the same degree. You must repent of the root of covetousness, which is idolatry (Col. 3:5), for in denying or demeaning men's blessings, you defame the one whose sovereignty assigned those blessings, God himself, thinking that you would have dealt more justly than he did. "Nay but, O man, who art thou that repliest against God? Shall the thing formed say to him that formed it, Why hast thou made me thus?" (Rom. 9:20).

Moreover, because race is real, so are racial besetting sins, and thus each race must be called to repent of them. We have previously discussed Black sins (see especially chapter 3, under "Morality"), and here we call Blacks to turn from them. Black men, you are my fellow human beings, but like the Cretians, you behave like evil beasts; therefore I must rebuke you sharply (Titus 1:12–13). You must repent of your gross fornication, your deeply broken families, your woeful criminality, and your wanton disregard for life, as in such shameful numbers you murder my own people, and especially your fellow Blacks. You must repent of your false form of godliness (2 Tim. 3:5), by which so many in your churches shout "Lord, Lord," but will be told on the last day, "Depart from me, ye that work iniquity" (Matt. 7:23). You must also repent of your willful participation as a tool of godless social revolution. You willingly assisted in the burning down of Christendom, in the American South, in Rhodesia, in South Africa. And what have you gained from it but guilt and shame, and deeper slavery to sin and misery? In all these things you must repent of your own racial pride, which cannot abide an honest assessment of your race's weaknesses and sins, especially from the lips of Whites.

Now we confess that being Black itself will not keep you from heaven: all from every nation who trust Jesus Christ and turn from sin are saved. But if pride in the blackness of your race keeps you from humiliation over the blackness of your soul, then you cannot be saved. God is no respecter of persons (Acts 10:34–35): he will cast unrepentant Blacks into "the blackness of darkness for ever" (Jude 13).

We leave to other non-White races to consider and repent of their own evils, and we turn to the besetting sins of Whites. I speak to my own brethren, my kinsmen according to the flesh: my natural affection for you calls me to an even deeper heartfelt sorrow for your manifold rebellion against God. White men, race realism testifies to blessings you've enjoyed above others. But it appears these blessings have puffed you up with godless pride. Our racial characteristics of virtue and intelligence, of exploration and invention, our inheritance of stable government, generational wealth, and global influence and power, are good, worthy of thankful celebration. But they are blessings merely natural, in themselves no proof of saving favor. Whatever Christian grace with which our White ancestors exercised their noble callings, their White sons today have fallen far from it. Without faith, without humility, without gratitude, our blessings have become our curses, and we abuse them by self-aggrandizement, love of money, gluttony, and senseless lust for pleasure. We choke upon our sumptuous food, and drown in the wine of our debauchery. Like the rich man in Luke 16, we have our good things in this life, but we will lose them all when we are sent to hell, while our racial inferiors who have hated sin and trusted Christ will go into the kingdom of God before us. O White man, you may rule on earth, but you will be a slave under the earth forever, if you will not repent.

I must continue with my people here. For in this age they have deeply degraded themselves by an unmentionably evil sin, that of suicidal despair. The prevailing anti-White hatred which stirred us up to write this series, has its worst form in White self-hatred. Of this deep evil, my dear kinsmen, you must deeply repent. Repent of joining our enemies in slandering our honorable fathers, calling their good deeds evil, exaggerating their real evils far out of proportion, and performing for the devil, flattering your conscience, and lying to God himself, by false repentance for false sins, falsely alleged against our race. Repent of taking the inheritance God gave to you, the lands you settled, conquered, and painstakingly cultivated, the wealth you earned by centuries of honest labor, and parceling it out to millions of strangers who hate you and your children. Repent of letting foreigners defy your borders, fill your neighborhoods, vote in your elections, rule your cities, and poison your bodies and your souls with foreign drugs and foreign vices. Repent of your refusal to marry women of your own, and to have children of your own, of your willful racial self-destruction by contraception and miscegenation. Repent, my fellow White men, most of all for your abandonment of the best part of our inheritance, the Christian faith, of your apostasy from Christ, the son of Shem into whose tents the sons of Japheth have been called to dwell (Gen. 9:27).

White men, in all these ways you have sinned not only against God, but against yourselves; not only against God's holiness, but also against his kindness: not just his kindness to all men, but his kindness to you in particular. O self-hating White men, why would you forsake your own mercies? Why like Esau so despise your birthright as to sell it for a pot of stew? We plead with you to cast away all your transgressions, and make you a new heart and a new spirit: for why will ye die, O house of Japheth?

4. Honor

Most of the positive application proper to the theme of race could be summed up in the fifth commandment, "Honor thy father and thy mother." For races are extended families, special bonds of blood which call accordingly for special honor. Those bonds are all the stronger as they are the closer, so honoring our race must begin by honoring our household. Children must honor their parents by obeying them, wives their husbands by submitting to them, husbands their wives by lovingly leading them, parents their children by nurturing and disciplining them. We suspect that most of our day's racial dysfunction is a product of familial dysfunction: as the family, so the nation, so the race. This can be a help to those who are overwhelmed at the large scale of racial issues today. Each individual may be at a loss to rescue his entire race, but by simply visiting his widowed grandmother, he plays a valuable part in that rescue.

Only on this foundation of filial piety may the duties to our broader relations be laid. We ought to flee the self-serving "virtue signal" of "telescopic philanthropy," as well as any form of nationalism that ignores those in our nation closest to us.

Yet still, though every furnace gives the most warmth to those nearby, the hotter the furnace, the more it will also cast its heat to those beyond. So for our love: the stronger it is, the more it will extend beyond our family, tribe, and clan, to our whole nation, and our race, and from there to all mankind. The true Christian especially, whose chief love is for God exalted in the heavens, ought to include all lesser earthly things as well within the compass of that love. So ought believers, of all men, not be indifferent toward their ethnic brethren, their kinsmen according to the flesh (Rom. 9:3). Those who honor God have every reason to honor their race.

5. Marriage

We dealt already with the question of inter-racial marriage in chapter 5, objection 9. Here it seems good to expand on three things by way of application.

First, we need especially in marriage to destroy the modern idol of individualism, and of libertarian free choice. The phrase "I'll do whatever I please" may have some usefulness in standing against radical communism, in which the individual is annihilated by amalgamation into the social mass, but it fails as a philosophy of life, spelling the ruin of families and nations. In marriage in particular, contrast the daughters of Zelophehad. In Numbers 27 the Lord commanded that, as their father had only daughters, they would receive his inheritance in order to maintain his name. However, in Numbers 36 came the concern that marrying into another tribe would remove that inheritance from their own. The Lord's command again solved the hard case: "Let them marry to whom they think best; only to the family of the tribe of their father shall they marry" (v. 6), which the daughters carefully obeyed (vv. 10–11). Their obedience is a rebuke to those today who would make their choice of spouse a matter of unfettered individual desire. These women did choose freely whom to marry, but they happily allowed that choice to be limited, even by strict law, according to what was best for their nation, their tribe, and their father's name and inheritance.

This example has relevance beyond the Old Testament. Marriage in any age is a union, not just of two individuals, but of two families, each of which form an organic part of a nation and a race. In principle each couple upon marrying binds their extended families to decades of life together, to weddings, funerals, reunions, graduations, and to the duties owed to future grandchildren, nieces, nephews, and cousins. Most families if asked would honestly prefer to have such fellowship within their race, even more narrowly within their nation. That couples today do not ask, is a shame. That they might ask, and are told no, but do it anyway, is further shame. Inter-racial marriages, now even decades after being decriminalized, are often still met with serious concerns expressed by family members. It's commonplace to dismiss such concerns as "racist" and unloving. But such dismissal is a fruit of individualism, and a breaking of the fifth commandment.

Second, we need to let our idealistic dreams be shattered on the rock of hard reality. The harmless, stable inter-racial marriage is a rare exception, more often a mere fiction, especially in marriages which seek to bridge the giant chasm fixed between White Europeans and Black Africans. The constant advertisements to the contrary are deceitful and demoralizing propaganda. Such marriages ignore the countless differences God himself established between the races of mankind—in color, features, height, health, custom, culture, food, place, politics, history, psychology, intelligence, morality, religion—only some of which can change within one lifetime, and most of those not drastically. Moreover, change in individuals does not mean change in their respective families or peoples; yet marriage is the joining of two families and peoples, as we saw.

This is not to mention the natural fruit of marriage, children. Inter-racial marriage sets large burdens on the shoulders of children who come from it—not belonging fully to either parent's race, stuck in a no-man's land of mounting racial conflict, at a disadvantage in their health and in their future marriage options—burdens which they never asked for, yet will have to bear throughout their lives, and pass on to some extent to their own children. This is especially so in White-Black marriages, because Black genetics usually express themselves so strongly in mixed offspring. Thus Whites who marry Blacks deal unkindly with their ancestors, by ending their centuries-long White genetic lineage, and with their future children, by in most cases passing on less intelligence than they would otherwise, and also by deciding for their children that, according to strong social custom, they will likely be treated Black and join with Black culture, and thus be subject to the constant threat of its degeneracy.

How can two young people face all these issues, and still think it's wise to charge ahead to marriage? Race realism would make them think more realistically.

Third, we must refuse to let our marriage be an instrument of godless social revolution. Yet inter-racial marriage has been such an instrument, at least in the United States, in two ways. First, it is a monument of the conquest of a political system foreign to our founding, as for over three hundred years our colonies and states had laws against mixed marriages. See chapter 4. Second, it was intentionally used as a stepping stone to the legal approval of perversion: *Obergefell v. Hodges* (2015, striking down bans on "gay marriage") drew intentionally upon *Loving v. Virginia* (1967, striking down bans on inter-racial marriage). Similarly, the so-called *Respect for Marriage Act* (2022) expressly aimed to uphold the validity of both same-sex and inter-racial marriage.

The revolutionary character of inter-racial marriage is also evident in Scripture, in which miscegenation is pictured as a tool of conquest. The Assyrians intentionally imported foreign men to erase the national identity of conquered Northern Israel (2 Kings 17:24). Moreover, God allowed an Israelite man to take a foreign female captive as a wife, provided that she shave her head, pare her nails, and "bewail her father and her mother a full month" (Deut. 21:11–13)—indicating that now their daughter, and part of their family line, was taken over by a total stranger.

In this, Scripture assumes male headship and patrilineal descent, that women in submitting to their husbands also assimilate together with their future children into their husband's people. This helps explain why most examples of mixed marriages in Scripture involve Israelite men taking wives from foreign women, not the other way around. When an Israelite daughter married a foreign man, the line of Israelite descent ended with her (cf. Lev. 24:10–11; 1 Kings 7:13–14; though see 1 Chron. 2:34-35).

The enemies of the White race, though most are feminists, still use this natural sexual dynamic to their advantage. By publicly placarding countless images of White woman with Black men, they project the conjugal conquest of White women as a means of securing total racial conquest over Whites. Add to this what we mentioned above, that even when a man is White and a woman Black, the dominance of Black genetics and power of social custom will strongly pull their children to re-assimilate into the Black race.

Finally, though we have had need to speak frankly here, we counsel care and patience when addressing those already in mixed marriages. We offer a help in our letter written to friends in inter-racial marriages as the first appendix of this book, which can give some ideas of how to speak with those who have already made a misstep in this matter.

We also would not unduly burden the consciences of those in unique circumstances. Some with just cause to be a racial sojourner may find themselves with need to marry, and with no nearby prospects from among their people; it appears to us this was the case with Joseph in Egypt, and Moses in Midian. Though do recall Isaac and Abraham's insistence that their sons take pains to find wives from their kin. Some may meet other barriers, like that of false religion, that make marrying within their race a practical impossibility. For all seeking to marry, race is by no means the only relevant question; as in so many other life decisions, wisdom considers countless factors, each according to their proper weight. We hope our treatment here gives help in this consideration.

6. Education

Children are the future, and their education shapes the future of their race. Therefore White families and White nations need to take a special care to instill in the White children a wholesome racial consciousness, and humble thankfulness for the blessings their race enjoys. Moreover, in education, we ought not fear racial segregation. Intellectual segregation is still known today, in dividing students by grades, and in special classes for the gifted, as is moral segregation, in schools that use detention and expulsion; less common but still practiced is religious segregation, in the Christian school. Why then do modern people balk at racial segregation? Especially since, because of the intellectual, moral, and religious differences between the races, the above forms of segregation often bring *de facto* racial segregation. Indeed such indirect forms of segregation, especially combined with the socio-economic segregation forced by large tuition bills in private schools, are often used by Whites in order to secure White-only schooling for their children, while not incurring the ire of the civil rights regime. We admire the shrewdness of this, but wish Whites did not have to act so clandestinely to preserve the interests of their children in their own countries. And we grieve that the price tags of private schools still leave many White children without this benefit.

Returning to *de jure* school segregation will bring great challenges, and call for great courage and wisdom, but we believe it would be worth the trouble. It would be best for White children, sparing them from physical and moral harm, better cultivating their unique gifts, and developing in them a wholesome racial consciousness. It would also be better for non-White children, as their particular needs would be able to be met more particularly. A witness to this are the "historically" (in truth, presently) Black colleges and universities throughout America, from which gifted Blacks may graduate with honor and go on to usefulness in their careers, while enjoying comfortable fellowship with their own people, whereas they would not have had the same success in a majority-White school, and would have been less comfortable as a minority. One example of the succesful contemporary implementation of racial segregation in education is the Movement for Christian Nationalist Education[60] in South Africa, an organization which manages a network of 30 mono-ethnic Calvinist schools which are currently being attended by 2,500 Boer children.

To Christians who object to this we offer the illustration of home-schooling, which many Christians happily embrace today. Is not one reason for this embrace a proper disgust at the depths to which the integrated schools have fallen? Are White home-schooling parents not happy that their children are insulated from constant encounters with racial strangers? And is not the home-school often celebrated precisely as it is the strictest form of racial segregation? There is no racial

---

60 "Beweging vir Christelik-Volkseie Onderwys," *Wikipedia: The Free Encyclopedia*, https://en.wikipedia.org/wiki/BCVO.

bond tighter than that of the immediate family. And by that bond the home-school mother and her children enjoy the welcome help of the strongest possible natural affection, because they have the strongest possible natural affinity. We argue here that the help of such natural affinity should also be embraced in racially-segregated schools outside the home.

7. Publishing

A people's reading shapes the people's minds, and so to change our people, we must change their books. Especially in Christian publishing, all "liberation theology," all "wokeness," all "critical race theory," and all half-measures toward those ends, like "colorblindness," need to be removed from all published literature. The books that have pushed these errors are so insidious, and bring such harm to all who read them, that we would not object to see them burned (cf. Acts 19:19). Especially insofar as churches have a say in the activities of Christian publishers, they ought to speak ecclesiastically against those who would so pollute their readers' minds, and cultivate such trouble in both church and state.

We add to this the cloying habit of pushing and praising non-White authors, simply because they are non-White. Of course it's easy for a publisher to deny hidden intentions, but most people have a natural sensitivity to "tokenism," and suspect it all the more in our day of "affirmative action." Moreover, it harms the very cause it aims to serve, as when readers discover that a non-White work is not up to the level of a work by Whites, they naturally develop doubt as to whether any non-White author is worth reading.

8. Politics

Here we must take more care and space, as politics is challenging, and can stir up the worst division. To help ourselves we distinguish between moral principles and their political applications, and in the latter between things that must be done and things that might be done, and in both of those, between things that will be done, and those that simply won't, whether they ought or not. We recognize that all political action will be naturally limited by circumstances, and by the will of leaders, and of their people. Given these distinctions, we call on readers to exercise patience and charity, not just here, but in all related political discussions. It is best to take strong political pronouncements with the above qualifications understood, even if not stated. So for example, in these matters many embrace the power of the slogan: "Mass Deportations Now!" "Foreigners Out!" "America for the Americans!" But such sloganeers should not be slandered as a politically inept, because their message is simple. Catchy "sound bites" can be the public face of careful jurisprudence, which would apply these slogans skillfully and patiently in discrete circumstances, under the guidance of trustworthy, sober civil leaders. This is how we intend our political statements to be taken here.

National Repentance

We begin with a principle that is spiritual, yet also inescapably political, that of national repentance. White nations like America need to recognize that the present threat to their White people is spelled out in Scripture as a national judgment:

The stranger that is within thee shall get up above thee very high; and thou shalt come down very low (Deut. 28:43).

Your country is desolate, your cities are burned with fire: your land, strangers devour it in your presence, and it is desolate, as overthrown by strangers (Isa. 1:7).

Our inheritance is turned to strangers, our houses to aliens (Lam. 5:2).

It may be the worst consequence of anti-race-realism, that White nations are not allowed to recognize themselves as nations, and thus are not allowed to see their own replacement by foreigners as a judgment of God, and thus are not moved to repent under that judgment. We plead with all White nations: God is judging you, by allowing foreigners to conquer you. Yes, those foreigners are sinning, and God will deal with them, but by them he is dealing with you, and if you will not repent, you will not survive. Where are the Canaanites today? The Americans, the English, the Germans, the Afrikaners will join them in total annihilation, if they as nations will not humbly bow before the Lord their judge, and kiss the Son of God (Ps. 2:12).

How does such national repentance happen? In Scripture, it is when the leaders of a nation, both ecclesiastical and civil, publicly confess the nation's sins, publicly call for mourning over them, often by decreeing solemn public fasts, and publicly commit to serve the Lord, often by the solemn swearing of a public national covenant. Excellent examples of this are evident in Ezra (ch. 9), Nehemiah (ch. 9), Hezekiah

(2 Chron. 29; 2 Kings 18), and Josiah (2 Chron. 34; 2 Kings 22–23), and outside Israel, in various kings (Dan. 3:29; 4:37; 6:26; Jon. 3), as well as in countless examples throughout the history of Western Christendom.

It does not appear that the leaders of today's White nations are anywhere close to such repentance. In that case, their people still have their duty. They must repent of sins as individuals, as families, as churches, and as smaller political communities, under the leadership of lesser magistrates. And they must pray for their people and their rulers, interceding as Moses did for Israel (Ex. 33), as Daniel for Judah (Dan. 9), even as Abraham for Sodom (Gen. 18). Those who do so ought to be encouraged by the promise of 2 Chronicles 7:14:

If my people, which are called by my name, shall humble themselves, and pray, and seek my face, and turn from their wicked ways; then will I hear from heaven, and will forgive their sin, and will heal their land.

Immigration

Here we summarize using a slogan mentioned above: "Foreigners Out!" We ought to recognize that for every nation, God has set the bounds of their habitation (Acts 17:27). This means that every nation has its proper home, including White nations, and as that home is theirs, it is their duty to keep it theirs, unless they would be conquered, enslaved, and destroyed.

We clarify that as in ancient Israel, so in modern nations, the foreign "sojourner" may have a place. But that place is as that of guest in someone else's home. Such is not the place of the majority of foreigners today, at least not in White nations: whether or not they came in first as guests, they now are treated as family, though it's obvious they aren't. Whether this new arrangement was our fault, or theirs, or both, it doesn't matter. It has to end, and quickly, for the good of the whole household, and its guests.

Practically this means, we must deport every single illegal immigrant, today, together with their families. To help this we should penalize those who employ them, reward those who report them, and as to the immigrants themselves, immediately cut off all their welfare benefits, and certainly not permit the madness of allowing them to vote in our elections. One of the most absurd benefits we give in America to foreign visitors is "territorial birthright citizenship," that their children, simply by birth on American soil, become American citizens.[61] It needs to end immediately. The common objection to deportation, "Who then will pick our vegetables?" is greedy and lazy. White men are capable of picking their own vegetables, and the greater food costs that may come from no longer paying illegals paltry wages "under the table," would be well worth the increase in our national unity.

But this is just a start. In America, very many "legal" immigrants are also a danger to our people, as they are neither able nor willing to assimilate into our founding stock of "White Anglo-Saxon Protestants." This was not at first a problem, as per our 1790 Naturalization Act only free White persons of good character were eligible to become citizens.

---

61   This article explains the matter well:
https://americanreformer.org/2024/08/the-end-of-birthright-citizenship/

19th-c. immigration through Ellis Island brought some serious changes to this, but the most drastic change came in 1965, with the passage of the *Hart-Celler Act*. The damage this act did to the makeup of America is incalculable. If our nation would survive, that act and all its consequences must be totally reversed. Some think it would be cruel to send back immigrants who were brought in under it, and now have lived for generations in America. But those immigrants still have their nations (indeed, many still visit them), and we have ours, to which by natural affection belongs our first and foremost duty. We should still practice humanity toward our long-term foreign guests, perhaps making the difficult move easier by paying them to leave, or otherwise encouraging voluntary repatriation, before turning to involuntary expulsion. But by whatever method, it is time for them to go. Foreigners Out!

Crime

Here is one place we ought to affirm "colorblindness." Justice is blind, strictly punishing all duly proven crimes without respect of persons. "One law shall be to him that is homeborn, and unto the stranger that sojourneth among you" (Ex. 12:49). Such impartial application of justice would help take the edge off racial conflict. For example, the death penalty is an appropriate, fitting, indeed biblical punishment for murder, rape, and adultery. Its diligent use would do much to stem the tide of violence by Black men and other violent foreigners. As would proportional strict punishment for theft and fornication, the latter having the additional benefit of reducing illegitimacy, and thus also of preventing children in America from being mixed-race, as per one study,[62] 92% of biracial children with Black fathers are illegitimate. If Blacks and their supposed supporters would condemn such justice as "racist," we should respond by doubling down on impartial enforcement, insisting that the proper way for Blacks to avoid prosecution, is by avoiding crime.

Segregation

Such impartiality does not, however, oppose legal racial discrimination upon reasonable grounds. On this see chapter 5, objections 13 and 14. It is no sin for the magistrate to recognize racial differences, and legislate according to them. In specific, it is no sin for magistrates to impose some measure of racial segregation, when circumstances warrant it. Recall from chapter 2 the various ways that God himself segregated Israel from other nations, especially the Canaanites, and compare chapter 5, objections 10 and 11.

A reasonable beginning here would be to remove all legal barriers to *de facto* racial segregation, and all free racial association. It is absurd that even in their own nations, Whites are forbidden from creating White-only neighborhoods, businesses, and schools. Even if their motive in doing so were only that they prefer their own people, the law should be no hindrance to this. But as we have seen, Whites have various more weighty reasons to seek separation from others,

---

62   https://www.researchgate.net/publication/
315367933_Ninety_Two_Percent_Examining_the_Birth_Trends_Family_S
tructure_Economic_Standing_Paternal_Relationships_and_Emotional_Sta
bility_of_Biracial_Children_with_African_American_Fathers

not least of which is the maintenance of their own safety and morality.

After this, wise rulers should at least consider measures of *de jure* segregation. For models of this they have not only the Mosaic civil law, but also at least three centuries of modern jurisprudence, from places like America where Protestant rulers encountered extreme racial differences, and dealt with them by imposing various forms of racial segregation, as explained in chapter 4.

We are aware how revolutionary these proposals sound. But properly they are not revolutionary, but "counter-revolutionary," as they aim to undo a prior overturning of nature and of wholesome civil law. We do not call for turning the world upside down, but right-side up. This will require enormous fortitude, as in the past, so all the more today, segregationists will have to nullify pronouncements of judiciaries, defy enactments of legislatures, and resist the bayonets of executives. But all true Christians already know this is the case in regard to other legalized evil, like abortion and "gay marriage." It should not surprise them therefore that the same resistance is required against miscegenation. After all, it is the same "civil rights" regime that brought upon us all these modern evils. The entire egalitarian revolution must be destroyed, root and branch.

Employment

In the business world, all "affirmative action" and "diversity, equity, and inclusion" programs should end immediately. Employers are abetting revolutionaries, harming customers, and destroying their own businesses, by intentionally employing the less qualified simply because they are "persons of color." Again, however, we do not oppose all racial preference in employment. White-only businesses should have their place. In a White country, it is natural and normal to prefer to give jobs to White fellow countrymen, even at the expense of a strict "meritocracy." For otherwise, under modern libertarian "free trade," and especially under the Hart-Celler Act, average White citizens face competition from the best and brightest of the entire globe. This is unfair, unkind, and unpatriotic. "American jobs for Americans" is a sound slogan here. This and other forms of economic protectionism flow naturally from natural affection.

Suffrage

Many in America today are waking up to the disaster that came from the 19th Amendment, securing women's suffrage. God gave women many gifts, but civil rule is not one of them; indeed, he mocks a people whose women rule over them (Isa. 3:12). Fewer see it, but the same is true of Black suffrage, enacted by the 15th Amendment. Like women, Blacks show themselves incapable of civil rule, inevitably becoming clients of their natural superiors, whether for good or ill. Today, it is most certainly for ill: Blacks vote solidly for Democrats, a party sounder in the past, but now a gross public promoter of impiety, perversion, murder, and "anarcho-tyranny." Unless we White men find strength to remove the franchise from those who cannot but abuse it, their votes will continue to harm our nation, and themselves. As we argued in chapter 5, objection 13, any civil right may be revoked if it does not serve the common good. But the Black vote by no means serves the common good.

Moreover, under Hart-Celler immigration, the 15th Amendment allows countless other racial strangers access to the voting booth. Indeed one reason our politicians permit them to invade our country by the millions, is to obtain a loyal voting bloc. White men are fools to think this will end well for them.

Self-defense

Many will balk at this suggestion, but we must also mention the possibility of violent racial conflict. Of all men, Christians must be men of peace: to love killing in itself, or to use it for anything other than necessary justice, shows a callous disregard for life. But so does a refusal to recognize when true justice demands taking up arms. What if with the power Whites still hold, we attempt as outlined above to restore racial order peaceably, but violent racial factions mobilize against us? Or what if Whites lose their power in their countries, and their new rulers order their execution? What if Americans are subject to our own Bolshevik or Haitian revolution, threatening our murder by the tens of millions? If in our land we hear the genocidal chants now heard throughout South Africa? Should we simply submit to slaughter? We answer in the clearest terms: *Not while we breathe*. If the question of White existence must be answered by White arms, far better to die fighting than to passively accept extinction. Self-defense is a most obvious duty of nature, and of the moral law under the sixth commandment, an inalienable right of individuals, families, and nations. The wise White man today already carries a weapon when he must be in the bad part of town. God forbid it, but if the whole town turns bad, or the whole country, he must be armed and ready, not only as a man, but as a race. To say such self-defense will never be necessary, or should never be used in any case, reveals an ignorance of history, an indefensible pacifism, and a suicidal self-hatred, which so besets the White man in our age, and from which we say again, he must repent.

9. Church

If care was needed in applying race realism to the civil polity, all the more is it needed in the ecclesiastical. For the church is "the house of God" and "the pillar and ground of the truth" (1 Tim. 3:15): if anywhere, then surely in the church, must nature, order, truth, and righteousness be honored and upheld.

Ministry

We begin with ministers, as they are Christ's gift "for the perfecting of the saints" (Eph. 4:12). And we are bound here to call them to repentance, for many in this matter have made themselves enemies to those same saints. Pastors of White congregations must cease their callous indifference to their own people's racial plight: to deny, downplay, or dismiss discussion of White genocide is heartless and discouraging, like saying to the naked and the hungry, "Depart in peace, be ye warmed and filled" (James 2:16). They must repent from tolerating, countenancing, and especially from inculcating "anti-racism," especially when in doing so they wrest the Scriptures (2 Peter 3:16; see chapter 5, objections 8, 10–12). We have seen ministers condemned by their own words, when they accuse the "kinist" of abusing Scripture, while boldly abusing it themselves to teach racial egalitarianism. They must repent of setting religious identity against national identity, or in particular, of using religion to entirely remove the racial character of national identity. They must stop treating "White nationalism" as heresy, but see instead that it is a lawful political conviction held by countless orthodox Protestants in history. Moreover, it is as American as apple pie (as shown in chapter 4), so when ministers condemn it, they are implying that no self-conscious "Heritage American" can be a Christian.

Moreover, in this and other matters, today's ministers have need to repent of cowardly refusal to have anything to do with "controversial" people, and of unkind insistence that all trouble that surrounds bold tellers of the truth is their own fault. They must repent of uncharitable dealing with such men, and for dismissing their ideas without study or consideration. Sadly, it appears that in matters of race, broad social consensus is enough to put certain opinions, even when held by sound Christians, beyond the pale of Christian conversation. This ought not be. Why should the world determine discourse in the church? John said, "The friendship of the world is enmity with God" (James 4:4), and Christ, "That which is highly esteemed among men is abomination in the sight of God" (Luke 16:15).

Finally, ministers today must repent of their repentance. Since the sixties American denominations have tripped over themselves to issue overtures against their "racist" past. But as we have argued at length, especially in chapters 4 and 5, the race realism of historic godly Christians was not sinful, and thus not to be repented of. It should deeply trouble any sincere gospel minister that he might have had a hand in inculcating false repentance for false sins. For calling for such false repentance brings great harm: in the righteous, it saddens hearts and strikes against assurance, and in the wicked, it breeds self-righteousness, hardens against true repentance, and therefore tends toward damnation. It is subject to the condemnation of Ezekiel 13:22, "With lies ye have made the heart of the righteous sad, whom I have not made sad; and strengthened the hands of the wicked, that he should not return from his wicked way, by promising him life." By promoting it, ministers of the gospel have, like Peter in Galatians 2:14, "walked not uprightly according to the truth of the gospel." And therefore other ministers, like Paul, ought to withstand them to their face (v. 11).

We realize the repentance we are calling for is very deep, and very difficult. It requires an admission that the best of our ministers, men otherwise sound and godly, have been either ignorant, or cowardly, or both, in that they have failed to address, even to recognize, a weighty moral issue of our day, and a deep compromise within the modern church, and moreover, that they have dismissed, demeaned, and even destroyed men who would have exposed their failure. This hurt cannot be healed slightly (Jer. 6:14).

As a help in assessing and addressing this widespread problem, we encourage all to read this 1648 deliverance from the Church of Scotland,[63] entitled, "Act for Censuring Ministers for their Silence, and not Speaking to the Corruptions of the Time."

Missions

Missions, both foreign and domestic, is without doubt a duty of the church of Christ, especially in the New Testament. But we also ought to realize that modern missions has become a major port of entry for egalitarian compromise. It is a common occasion for miscegenation, sometimes excused for the sake of winning foreigners, though we judge that taking a foreign people's women in marriage, and otherwise threatening the borders of their national identity, is unlikely to win them. It is a frequent excuse for mass foreign immigration, often under color of taking in "refugees" and "asylees," though many today who claim that status lie, and even in cases of real need, one country cannot take on all the "huddled masses" of the world. Even among the truly needy, the first duty of a White nation is toward its own, and then toward other Whites, yet "refugee ministry" tends to serve mostly non-Whites, and by its nature, only foreigners. There is a proper place for serving foreigners, but we are not convinced most of such ministries hold such a place. One reason is, they never seem to offer a critique of modern immigration, except when such critique calls for White

---

63 https://www.thedailygenevan.com/blog/2021/1/14/
    CensuringForSilence1648

borders to be opened further. Another is, they never seem to tell the migrants to go home, though for most of today's migrants, going home would be the path of true repentance and true righteousness. To all appearances, and despite all good intentions, many of these ministries serve to the harm of their nations and their churches, and even to the refugees themselves, bring less spiritual good than advertised. Some of these ministries are deeply subversive, a Christian "fifth column" serving the modern racial revolution, and ought to be dealt with as such.

As regards priorities in missions, we recall the image of a furnace, which when warmer casts it heat the further, but still gives its best heat to those nearby. The church has a duty to teach all nations (Matt. 28:19; Mark 16:15), but not every positive duty is to be done at every time, in every way and degree, by everyone. In White nations today, our people languish spiritually; churches are few and far between, especially outside our cities, and in America, outside the "Bible Belt." The churches we do have are weak, with countless nigh to death; many have already had their candlestick removed, and now are synagogues of Satan. With our people in such a state, it betrays a lack of natural affection, bordering on spiritual cruelty, to send off many of our best to foreign lands, while our own people hurtle by the millions into hell. Compare the famous 19th-century foreign missions movement: one condition of its success was the flourishing of Protestant Christendom in the sending countries. We cannot say that it is flourishing today in those same countries. Until it is, it is fitting for foreign missions not to be as high of a priority.

Again, we do not deny the duty of foreign missions. Nor would we say it should entirely cease today, or that no man is right to feel and heed a call to it. We simply insist on the wise application of natural affection in the discernment of this call. Like Christ weeping over Jerusalem (Luke 9:41), Paul was in anguish for the lost condition of his "kinsmen according to the flesh" (Rom. 9:3). God did still send him as the "apostle of the Gentiles" (Rom. 11:13), and he was right to go. But the book of Acts demonstrates the care Paul took still to evangelize his countrymen. Even as we long for all the nations to rejoice in Christ, we ought all the more long to see such joy return to our own nations. We believe the fields are "white to harvest" in White nations, and we pray therefore to the Lord of the harvest, that he will send forth laborers into them (John 4:35; Matt. 9:38).

Segregation

The "anti-racist" revolution has put churches in a hard place. The church ought never countenance social and political disorder, but neither does it have the calling or the power to remove it altogether on its own. "If the foundations be destroyed, what can the righteous do?" (Ps. 11:3). A stable commonwealth is a normal precondition for a stable church: thus the church is to pray "for kings, and for all that are in authority; that we may lead a quiet and peaceable life in all godliness and honesty" (1 Tim. 2:2).

Therefore in our disordered day, we are reluctant to lay down specific rules regarding racial segregation in the church. In chapter 5, objections 7 and 8, we affirmed the propriety of such rules, in principle, in fitting circumstances, such as those under which past orthodox churches practiced segregation. But this is not the same as requiring those same specific rules today. For one thing, all those churches practiced segregation in a society in which such segregation was common outside church, and in many places still enforced by law.

We do not say this to forbid all forms of racial segregation in the church today. Indeed, because the church cannot countenance social disorder, it has all the more reason to stand against a society the more that society is disordered. We only mean to emphasize that prudent dealing here requires great wisdom, patience, courage, and even godly ingenuity, all in ways specifically appropriate to each specific circumstance. We therefore cannot dictate what each church should do. But as a help in their discernment, we believe we can speak clearly on three things.

First, churches ought to embrace *de facto* racial segregation without shame. There is nothing wrong, at all, with churches that are entirely White (or for that matter, entirely Black, entirely Brown, etc.). It is a natural result of natural affection: men of the same sort like to live, to socialize, even to worship with each other. The church has absolutely no business forcing this to change. Indeed, as shown by the example of Dutch immigrant churches (given in chapter 5, objection 7), it has sound reasons to embrace it as a positive good, and a natural help to the fulfillment of its spiritual purposes.

Second, churches ought at least to recognize the difficulties that can come when racial strangers join a church. A small number of foreign visitors, perhaps even foreign members in special circumstances, especially in larger churches, will likely cause no trouble. If civil Israel could entertain the sojourner, why not the spiritual Israel, the church of Christ? Yet as in the civil household, so in the ecclesiastical, when foreigners are present in such numbers, or in such a manner, that the stranger threatens harm to the native, then problems come.

Take especially the case of Black visitors in White churches in America. Blacks have now for over a century and a half been used by unscrupulous politicians as a tool to harm the White majority. Their crime rates are proverbial, and their own hatred of the White man often public and virulent. Many Whites have worked hard to avoid proximity to Blacks, including moving from the city to the suburbs, or from the suburbs to the country. So it is natural that they feel concern when Blacks appear in the next pew in their White church. Add to this that in our climate White men fear they cannot express this concern; indeed that if they do, it is they who will be promptly segregated from the church. Ministers and elders ought not despise their members for thinking this way, and ought do all they can to help allay their fears.

We do recall the example of past Southern churches with both Blacks and Whites in membership, and recognize that this is not entirely impossible. Yet we also recall the terms of that arrangement were not racially egalitarian, as neither were the terms of Black-White fellowship outside the church. So we doubt, even if resuming this past practice were desirable, that it would be fitting to our circumstances, or acceptable to all involved.

Third, churches never should countenance any rule, regarding race or otherwise, that compromises biblical principles, or betrays the gospel that the church must preach. Recall from chapter 5, objection 8, that Peter's racial segregation in Galatians 2 was a sin precisely because it denied justification by faith alone. Insofar as any segregation today would so deny the gospel, we would strongly oppose it. We are sympathetic here to those who fear giving the appearance of such evil, and thus would never make any rule regarding race in church. Yet we counsel caution: the critical interpretation of a hostile world, or of a corrupt and worldly church, is not the rule of our obedience. Ministers need courage today to do what's right, not what is merely popular, what best glorifies God and edifies Christ's church, not what best avoids the criticism of the world.

Ordination

We see no reason why, by grace, at least some men from every race could not be qualified and called to gospel ministry, according to the rules given in 1 Timothy 3 and Titus 1. Nor do we see why churches of various races would not recognize and honor each other's ordinations. This is presently done between churches in different countries, and is a sweet confirmation of their spiritual unity in Christ. But this does not mean it is usually prudent for ministers of one race to serve members of another, at least in a stated, regular capacity.

Compare here the barrier of language. A minister who cannot speak a people's language, cannot serve them, at least not without the burden of interpretation, which precludes regular stated ministry. Even a thick foreign accent is too great a burden for most church members. Racial differences often bring such language differences; if not, then still like language, race presents a natural barrier to ministry. Compare all the differences it usually brings with it, outlined in chapter 3.

In particular, we cannot see how it would ever be wise to appoint a Black minister over a White church. In chapter 4 we saw that R. L. Dabney opposed the same in his own day, and we believe his reasons still apply to ours. As a general rule, Blacks are intellectual inferiors to Whites, but ministers, according to their duties, and the respect owed to their office, should be their people's intellectual superiors. To appoint the weak to rule the strong is kind to neither: both will suffer. Indeed we fear one reason so many Black ministers in White churches are so subversive today, is that they are given responsibilities beyond their actual abilities, which flatters them and makes them proud. We would add that a Black man truly qualified for ministerial office is a rare blessing in our day, and that the most fitting use of his unique gifts would be in service to his own people, who stand in serious need of them. What a blessing it would be to see a sound Black church, taught by solid Black ministers. May the Lord grant this in his mercy.

Yet though the principle of civil kin-rule (Deut. 17:15) has an analogical application to the visible church, we must add that there could be exceptional circumstances in which a White minister or elder might be appointed serve in a Black church, at least for a season. For the same reasons of intellect, Whites are able to lead Blacks in a way Blacks cannot lead Whites. And there is no necessary threat to racial boundaries if the White minister is careful to preserve them. Blacks themselves in the past understood the propriety of this, which is why so many of them gladly sat under the preaching of John Girardeau at Zion Church in Charleston, South Carolina (mentioned in chapter 5, objection 11). Given the sad state of Black Christianity today, we do not know if the Black church can be revived without such godly White missionary-pastors sent again to win Black souls.

Something similar is understood in foreign missions today: America sends missionaries to Africa or Asia, but receives almost none back from them, and few complain, or think this is an insult to the Africans and Asians, or to the Americans. Rather, it is both sensible and compassionate. God granted the sons of Japheth enormous blessings spiritual and temporal above the other races, and they are therefore bound to exercise this racial superiority for the other races' good. Non-Whites need White leadership, even in spiritual things, and we are heartless to ignore this need because of a self-hating false humility.

Church Planting

We believe that in these pages we have spoken the truth regarding race. But we must face the fact that there are very few churches today where such truth is even tolerated, much less taught. Practically speaking, the behavior of its opponents in many cases threatens race realists with exile from present churches, no matter how godly or orthodox the race realists themselves may be. What then are they to do?

Reiterating what we counseled in point 2 above, the best we can, we should serve patiently within the present churches, showing all due submission to their present leadership, remembering that Christ counseled submission even to the Pharisees of his own day (Matt. 23:2), and that we must not forsake assembling (Heb. 10:25). Now, we ought not be naïve in this—Micah warns us, "Put ye not confidence in a guide" (Micah 7:5), and the Bereans tested even the apostles by the Scriptures (Acts 17:11)—but neither should we be uncharitable, impatient, or rebellious. Recall that race realism is not revolutionary, but rather, counter-revolutionary.

Even heeding all this counsel, some will be forced to leave their churches. Indeed, many already have been. Many, whether safely in a church or not, are wondering, What's next? Is it the time to plant new churches that openly embrace race realism?

We say, With God's help, yes it is. If only because it's always time to plant new churches, and race realism is true, and we should always plant churches that teach only what is true.

But we would give a warning here, that a church attempting to unite on race realism alone, will fail. As we have shown, it is a matter that touches on points of religion, and is confirmed by passages of Scripture. But in itself, it is a matter largely natural, social, and political. By itself it is no foundation for church fellowship, though we are well aware that error in regard to race tends to the harm of the foundation, and to the fellowship built on it.

Therefore if such churches will be built, they must be built upon the only solid ground, God's Bible and Christ's Gospel, "the apostles and prophets, Jesus Christ himself being the chief corner stone" (Eph. 2:20). Many churches today that have compromised on race, did so only after they abandoned this foundation. Others who appear to keep the main things sound, but still are racially egalitarian, do threaten that foundation, because they cannot but corrupt the meaning of certain parts of Scripture. Moreover, even if a church is right on race, it still can be heretical by departing from the Word in other ways, which would bring shame both to the name of Christ, and to the cause of race realism.

So the dangers and difficulties are manifold. But from this we ought not lose heart. For our encouragement, we should remember we are not the first to have this struggle. In chapter 4 we cited the founding "Address to All the Churches" of the Presbyterian Church in the Confederate States of America. These godly men also were persecuted for race realism. They believed the African slavery practiced in their region was founded and maintained in part upon real racial difference, even real racial inequality, and they manfully defended their race realism, even while in part because of it they suffered men's reproach, expulsion from their formerly united church, a bloody war, and sad defeat. But their labor was not at all in vain. The Southern Church was home to some of the greatest Christian ministers America has ever seen, men like Thornwell, Dabney, Girardeau, and Palmer, whose names are held in honor today even by those who oppose race realism. Their church maintained a faithful witness in its sound Protestant doctrine, simple purity of worship, and godly zeal for souls of every race. And even as the statues of the Southern heroes fall today, the literary monuments of the Southern Presbyterians remain, a testament to the possibility, and the beauty, of a race-realist Christian church.

May Christ himself build such a church today, and make us his willing servants in that building.

Appendix I:
Letter to Friends in
Inter-Racial Marriages

Dear Friends,

I'm writing because you may have heard, or may hear soon, about my views on race, and I wanted you to hear them directly from me.

In short, I am a "race realist." This means I believe that though there is one human race, the more common use of the term race (to describe categories of ethnicity like Black, White, and Asian) speaks of something real. I affirm that the differences among such races are not only real, but largely permanent, and that races therefore are not interchangeable or replaceable.

Moreover, I gladly embrace and celebrate these realities as part of God's wise design for mankind, per Acts 17:26, "…and hath made of one blood all nations of men for to dwell on all the face of the earth, and hath determined the times before appointed, and the bounds of their habitation." Compare the division of the nations in Genesis 9–11, and the summary of it given in Deuteronomy 32:8. Racial diversity is part of God's good providence toward man, and ought to be honored and protected as such.

Now, I don't think race is everything. Differences in religion, for example, have much more weight for this life and the next. But race is not therefore nothing. Recognizing racial difference has important practical consequences for this life. We ought to follow God's design for mankind and not rashly mix what he has made distinct.

Among other things this means I believe inter-racial marriage is usually unwise. I recognize that you are in an inter-racial marriage, thus this letter. As you can testify, I've never disrespected you for this, or suggested that your marriage is invalid, though I have held these views for years. You freely chose to swear to a lawful covenant of marriage before God, and I intend with God to give all honor to that covenant, and to do all I can to help you gladly keep its terms.

However, this does not mean I think you made the best choice you could have. All recognize a key to marital success is compatibility, and that the challenges of having a good marriage, especially in our godless days, are so great, that we ought not add unnecessary burdens of our own accord.

I'm willing to weigh potential exceptions, but it seems in nearly every case, inter-racial marriage is such a burden. By it we intentionally choose to combine two races continents apart in origin, with significant differences in appearance, culture, language, even religion. By it we conjoin not just two persons, but two entire lineages, which in most cases to that point had been separate for thousands of years. Their families now by virtue of the choice their children made are compelled to interact, and every time they do, they must labor to cross all the barriers God himself set up between their races. In the case of international marriages this requires expensive and lengthy travel, not to mention passports, visas, customs, immigration, and so forth.

Think also of the consequences for the children. Children of parents different in race, by no choice of their own, come into the world with burdens on their back. Their parents were strangers to their spouse's race, but at least belonged to their own. Yet the children don't quite belong to any race at all. Their friends will be part of some distinct race (most all men are), but they will not. By appearance, by accent, by custom, and by parentage, they'll stick out like sore thumbs, which no child wants to do.

Moreover, as they mature they'll make a choice as to which race they will identify most with. By God's design this will usually be that of their father, but in reality this is not always so. Either option will bring difficulties, and naturally disappoint the parents whose race they did not choose. Think also then of their own marriages: they will be forced, again by no choice of their own, to be in some sort of inter-racial marriage themselves. But who will be willing to enter such a marriage with them? Most people, though they may fear saying it publicly, prefer to marry within their race. And if the children do find suitable spouses, their children will be born with burdens similar to what they bore, burdens that can only be totally removed by generations of intentional assimilation. And all these decades of burden will come upon dozens of offspring through the generations, simply because two of their forbears chose an inter-racial marriage.

I pass by medical issues more likely to occur among children of a mixed marriages, and reputable studies revealing how the above undesirable outcomes are not theoretical, but real, and common.

However, I must add that all these challenges are greatly compounded in our day by an undeniable political reality: inter-racial marriage is especially promoted by godless liberals who seek the ruin of the White Christian nations that have historically been their strongest opponents. In the United States, legal barriers to it which had been in place since the colonial era were not repealed in all the states until the sixties (a moral low-point in our history), and that only after a century of ceaseless racial agitation, even violent revolution.

I do not attribute to you such malicious politics. But still you ought to recognize, in most places in our country, within the memory of our grandparents, your marriage would not have been approved of socially. In many states it would have simply been illegal. Moreover, in that day the opposition to it would have come largely from Christians, and from both races involved, whereas the minority that approved it would have been, not without warrant, viewed as godless, rootless social activists.

Your marriage despite your best intentions has been a fruit and instrument of that activism. Consider the fact that the left intentionally used the legalizing of inter-racial marriage as a stepping stone to legalizing homosexual marriage. I know you want no part in that, and I grieve with you that evil men abuse your marriage for these evil ends. But this is our political reality. Moreover, this is why I am compelled, as a Christian in our present circumstances, to promote and defend truth on this matter publicly, no matter what cost may come to me for it.

Again, I do not say these things to invalidate your marriage. I love you, your spouse, and your children. I affirm your lawful marriage, and as I always have, I will continue to support you in it. I furthermore am happy to help you all I can in navigating whatever particular difficulties may come to you and to your children because of it. I remain your loyal friend and thank the Lord for you, and for your marriage.

Moreover, I trust that we confess together, whatever wisdom we may have lacked in our past choices, they are real and irreversible, and ultimately they happened by the immutable choice of God's own all-wise providence, to which we all ought humbly to submit, and which always works for good to them that love him.

I fear some will try to misrepresent my views to you. You might have concerns or fears about them yourself. So it seemed good to be frank and open to you here. I'm happy to talk further if you desire.

Yours Sincerely in Christ,
Michael Spangler

Appendix II:
Response to Pastor Douglas Wilson

On July 17, 2024, Pastor Douglas Wilson wrote a reply to chapter 1 of this book (originally published as an article) on Christian race realism, entitled "The Shimmering Unreality of Race Realism." We respond here against his arguments, showing that they contain various absurdities, and veer into some serious unkindnesses, but that his postscript does offer some hope for the cause.

Absurdities

The substance of Pastor Wilson's main argument is that because racial boundaries are somewhat fuzzy, race realism is not true. In my article I spoke of racial differences as "relatively permanent," and I say that race is "practically" immutable, because there are peripheral cases, and races do change somewhat over the long term. He says my concessions spell the ruin of the entire cause. For example,

If ethnogenesis is possible in the short term, and for every young earth creationist it mostly certainly is, then stick a fork in race realism. It's done.

We note already that his terms need stricter definition. I granted in my article that "new races may form by ethnogenesis," as for example in the separation of the three sons of Noah (Gen. 10:32). But now thousands of years after that, it seems most racial development we observe is more modest and limited. What we describe as "ethnogenesis" is usually no more than the development of a distinct nation within one race. For example, the American Revolution helped forge the English majority and the various other Northwestern European ethnic minorities in the colonies into, in John Jay's words, "one united people":

> With equal pleasure I have as often taken notice, that Providence has been pleased to give us this one connected country to one united people—a people descended from the same ancestors, speaking the same language, professing the same religion, attached to the same principles of government, very similar in their manners and customs, and who, by their joint counsels, arms, and efforts, fighting side by side throughout a long and bloody war, have nobly established general liberty and independence.

But note Jay's assumption of a pre-existing descent "from the same ancestors." Contrast this to our African slaves, who struggled with us through the same war but were not amalgamated in the heat of same furnace into "one united people" with us, though we could rightly say that through their own particular furnace they were forged into a distinct ethnicity within the Black race, "African-Americans." Note how in these two cases "ethnogenesis" did not at all disturb the boundaries of larger racial categories. Just as the parallel

Wilson implicitly draws on, speciation (more on young earth creationism below), did make canines diversify into wolves and foxes and domestic dogs, but presently does not remove those now long-fixed distinctions, just as it does not remove the created distinction of "kind" between all canines and all felines.

However weak this argument from ethnogenesis, the others are embarrassingly more so. For example, he says,

A black man could easily have a great-grandchild, bearing his last name and everything, within his lifetime, descended from his loins, who could easily pass for a native-born Norwegian.

Is it not obvious that this example *assumes* the race realism it sets out to disprove? In this case the identifiably Black man has identifiably White great-grandchildren, precisely because he intentionally replaced most his Black genetics by successive generations of miscegenation. The racial reality has not changed, the boundaries between Black and White have not changed; rather, one man, together with generations of his offspring, has labored intentionally to cross those boundaries. The countless millions of Blacks and Whites who did not do this with him still remain just as Black and just as White as before he set out on his transgenerational, transcontinental journey of racial immigration. And once his own great-grandchildren have "become White," that's what they are, which again reaffirms that White and Black are really different.

The above example is plausible, though it proves nothing against race realism. However, a later hypothetical example leaves the realm of plausibility entirely:

*And so if we put 500 single blacks and 500 single whites on a deserted island the size of Tahiti, and we ensured that they were all Christians, all spoke English, and were all demographically similar in other ways, and we left them there for some 500 years, when we came back to see what had happened, the thing most likely to have changed would be this very thing that Spangler is calling immutable—what he calls race. They would still be speaking English, with their own accent certainly, they would still likely be Christian, at least formally, and they would all be a color that was **not** one of the two originals. Race is not immutable.*

The unreality of this hypothetical is manifold, and dare we say, "shimmering." Besides the fact that few sane Whites or Blacks would even assent to such a strange experiment, the qualifiers "all Christian" and "all spoke English" make false tacit assumptions, namely that they would be the same sort of Christians, and speak the same sort of English. We would ask, where in America can you find five hundred Blacks and five hundred Whites who are religiously compatible enough to marry prudently? Or five hundred who would not have to resort to perpetual "code switching" to speak in a dialect not considered strange to their hypothetical inter-racial partner? This is not to mention the countless other ways in which Whites and Blacks are not "demographically similar." Yet these are small problems, relatively. The glaring false assumption of the scenario is, that even with those other things all somehow being equal, the Whites and Blacks would even have the desire to marry each other. My generation of White men grew up well after *Loving v. Virginia*. Black-White marriage was daily set before our eyes by zealous social propagandists. Many of us had daily close social interactions with Black people. Yet statistically, we still almost never married them. We simply were not interested. To assume the likelihood that this would change drastically, even on that strange imaginary island, asks too much of any thinking reader.

But even if we granted this implausible scenario resulting in the implausible conclusion of a perfectly mixed new Black-White island tribe, so what? We've already affirmed that ethnogenesis is possible, and that it doesn't deny race realism. The millions of Whites and Blacks not on the island would remain just as White and Black as ever. We'd have a new small nation, call it a very small new race, but even so, both it, and the races it was formed from, would be just as real as ever.

I can't address all the other examples of absurdity in Wilson's article, but a few more should make it clear. One is this specious claim:

But as our knowledge of genetics has grown, the very rudimentary conceits of the early 20th century racialists can now be found on that now overcrowded ash heap of history. Human beings from all ethnic backgrounds are 99.9% the same. And the differences that strike us as being so "total," like skin color, are the result of differences in 0.01% of our DNA.

This should barely need refuting. Yes, the difference in DNA among mankind is found in a relatively small portion of our genetic code. But this does not argue in the slightest against the fixed racial differences which common sense observes. It simply means the DNA that accounts for those differences does not take up much space. Humans and chimpanzees share up to 99% of DNA. Should we therefore deny "species realism," and push for a revolution in inter-species relations, a "civil rights movement" to grant total social equality to the rest of the great apes? Of course not, nor do we think Pastor Wilson would say otherwise.

I pass over the reference to "skin color," which throughout he uses as a synonym for race, to make the race-realist position look ridiculous. This also is absurd, and quite unfair. Skin color is important, but not the most important racial difference. Like a jersey, skin color helps identify a racial "team," but has little to say about the manner in which that team plays the game.

We already considered the earlier example of the intentionally miscegenating Black man. Wilson apparently finds this sort of argument compelling, as he later goes on to make as much as possible of various "impossible tangles" that come from racial mixing. He mocks the "one drop rule" used in some earlier American jurisprudence, but fails to offer a solid alternative for how our courts may best define the boundary of Black and White, though this remains relevant for legal purposes even under "civil rights." He then says,

Researchers have also found that when people have less than 28% African ancestry, they tend to identify as European-American. And this is not all that hard to do, depending. I have an acquaintance whose grandfather was born a black Roman Catholic in New Orleans, and died a white Lutheran in Ohio.

All he has identified here is that, at some point through miscegenation Black genes are sufficiently replaced by White genes that the offspring count as White. Again, this assumes fixed racial boundaries. The most the strange case of this acquaintance's grandfather can prove is that such racial migration has a midpoint where it can be hard to tell which side of the line a certain man is on. But this assumes the line is there.

We note that the man's identity as possibly both "Black" and "White" is just asserted. Some observers may have found the man more obviously one or the other. But if we grant this one man could convince all others that he could be either Black or White, still, such a man would be exceedingly rare —"one in a million" would be underestimating it. And to use this odd wayfaring racial stranger as a proof that Black and White are not fixed racial categories is, again, absurd. As absurd as standing on the beach, seeing the wet sand, the crashing waves, the moving tide, and arguing from this that our prior assumption of a real, fixed boundary between the land and sea was hasty, yea "both manifestly and dangerously false."

This absurdity is as glaring as it is tiring. But in our day it is also a huge liability. We cannot ignore the formal similarity of Wilson's arguments to other more sinister claims. For example, take the "intersex," those who through no fault of their own, by chromosomal or anatomical abnormalities, are born with some sexual ambiguity. "Transgender" advocates argue from this exceeding rarity that sex is fluid, and men can become women. We do not attribute this perverted argument to Pastor Wilson. But we do challenge him to reckon with the fact his arguments about race take the same tack: arguing from strange cases at the edge of natural boundaries in order to deny those very boundaries exist.

If Wilson will not hear us on this point, we beg that he would hear his "favorite papist,"[64] G. K. Chesterton (quoted here[65] from "The Patriotic Idea"):

> Lastly, if he says, as he certainly will, that it is unreasonable to draw the limit at one place rather than another, and that he does not know what is a nation and what is not, we shall say: "By this sign you are conquered; your weakness lies precisely in the fact that you do not know a nation when you see it. There are many kinds of love affairs, there are many kinds of song, but all ordinary people know a love affair or a song when they see it. They know that a concubinage is not necessarily a love affair, that a work in rhyme is not necessarily a song. If you do not understand vague words, go and sit among the pedants, and let the work of the world be done by people who do." It is better occasionally to call some mountains hills, and some hills mountains, than to be in that mental state in which one thinks, because there is no fixed height for a mountain, that there are no mountains in the world.[66]

Unkindnesses

Wilson began his article with the ominous warning we already saw, that one of my central claims is "both manifestly and dangerously false." He then is more conciliatory about some agreements, and says, "I think we can talk about this

---

64 Douglas Wilson, "My Favorite Papist," *Blog & Mablog*, December 30, 2005. (https://dougwils.com/books-and-culture/s21-atheism-and-apologetics/my-favorite-papist.html).

65 Michael Hunter, "Natural Communities," *The Daily Genevan*, December 13, 2022.

66 G. K. Chesterton, "The Patriotic Idea," in *England: A Nation—Being the Papers of the Patriots' Club*, ed. Lucian Oldershaw, London and Edinburgh: R. Brimley Johnson, 1904, pp. 11–12.

without anybody freaking out." Though recent experience has shown this statement to be true only if the subject "we" is judiciously narrowed, I do share in his hope that God's grace is sufficient for brothers in Christ to learn to have productive, charitable discussion on this matter. But I cannot grant that this is what Wilson's article has done, or helped others to do. For besides the concerns mentioned above, certain things he says are also lacking in Christian kindness, as they strongly condemn fellow Christians without sufficient evidence.

We would not ourselves be unkind to Wilson by this claim. We are not speaking here of disagreements plainly stated, or sharply defended. Nor do we speak simply of public warnings against public error, which when warranted, are necessary. We speak rather of three things, two stated, the other left unsaid.

The first unkindness is his insinuation that race realists are implicit Darwinists. We saw already how he flashed his "young earth creationist" credentials. He later goes on a tangent about how long it might have taken for the "Ethiopian" (Jer. 13:23) to develop his distinctive skin, calculating at most 79, and at least 10 generations, which is either "short term" or "really short term." Besides the fact that this contributes to his false equation of race and skin color, why would he assume we disagree that a population could develop black skin within 10 generations? All I assert is that change within a race usually takes place slowly enough that we don't see it in our lifetime. I even grant that by God's unexpected intervention racial change can happen in one generation, though I would not assert particular instances of this without evidence, or make empirical generalizations according to this speculative possibility. Nor if it happened would it prove racial boundaries are fluid: if Asians tomorrow all somehow developed blue skin, they'd still be Asian, not White, and not Black, though "yellow" might become officially retired as a racial nickname.

Prior to this, Wilson draws the connection with Darwinism more clearly:

Because of the passion for "scientific" categorization in the early 20th century, and under the hegemonic sway of Darwinism, all the smart people began classifying us in "racial" categories. We had always known about tribes, but it was not until the 20th century that people started measuring the width of our foreheads with calipers. ...

Racialism and attacks on racism are both products of this mentality. One glorified the distinctions between the races, ranking them hierarchically like dutiful Darwinists, and the other attacked such distinctions as being at odds with the rising egalitarianism. But in the first half of the 20th century, the racialists were still riding high, a trend that continued until old Adolph kind of ruined the eugenics party.

We pass by the gratuitous connection of our position to that of Adolph Hitler, which strikes us as a cheap leftist tactic. But honestly, saying "racialism" is a "product of this mentality," i.e. Darwinism, simply because we also assert fixed racial categories, and some measure of racial inferiority and superiority, is not any more equitable. It must be proven, not asserted, and certainly not merely insinuated.

I know well the arguments between Young Earth Creationists and Darwinists, about the speed of speciation, about "millions of years," about Genesis 1–2 and 9–11, about biblical chronology, and so forth. I myself stand firmly in the former camp on all these points, as do most of the race realists I know personally, as do the historic race realists which I commend, men like Jonathan Edwards and R. L. Dabney. Pastor Wilson will have to find a better argument to make us all into closet Darwinists. Until he does, these insinuations are not charitable.

The second unkindness follows up with an implication of the first, that race realists have replaced the gospel. Wilson states in various ways that the undeserved gift of widespread Christianization was a massive boon to the culture of the West. We agree with this. But in context of that argument he states, a bit coyly, but not unclearly:

This has led some to confuse the effect with the cause, but that's all right. They want to treat whiteness as the gospel, while their counterparts, the dumb people on the other side, want to treat whiteness as though it were the devil.

Who are the "some," the "they," who want to "treat Whiteness as the gospel"? They are the "counterparts" of "the dumb people on the other side." A few sentences later he makes clear who these two sides are:

In this moment, the CRT commies are preaching their false universal, while the race realists are telling us that we can find secure footing in our tribal particularities.

So Wilson is saying "race realists" "treat Whiteness as the gospel." No matter how cute the rhetoric, this is tantamount to saying, race realists are heretics. He gives his readers the choice between "Whiteness" and "the gospel," then implies race realists have made the choice for Whiteness, and therefore that they have rejected the gospel.

We defend ourselves against this charge by two arguments. First, simply stated, we are not heretics. As mentioned above, we stand in this matter with some of the most orthodox and godly Christian ministers who ever lived. In our article which Wilson is replying to, we say nothing heretical at all, and rather assert the contrary: "Race realism is no excuse for error, sin, or schism," an admonition which Wilson himself mentioned positively in his first paragraph. As to the specific claim, that we have chosen Whiteness over the gospel, we said the exact opposite in no uncertain terms:

Race does not have ultimate importance. Heavenly things, God, Christ, the gospel, faith, hope, love, and so forth, are far more excellent. Grace excels race as far as heaven excels earth. Racial religious privileges are real, and can be a help unto salvation—God works in families, nations, and generations— but they never in themselves saved anyone. Paul, for example, speaks in this way of the privileges of Jews in Romans 9:1–8. There will be no ancestry test to enter glory: the sole criterion of the last judgment will be "faith which worketh by love" (Gal. 5:6).

We note that Wilson just said in another blog article,[67] "The first rule of debate is that you should be able to state your opponent's position in terms that he himself would own, and then undertake to answer that." We say, "Physician, heal thyself."

Second, Wilson's argument rests on a false foundation, namely that all that has made "the West" (i.e., White Christendom) to be great, is the gospel.

---

67 https://dougwils.com/books-and-culture/s7-engaging-the-culture/a-rejoinder-to-internet-randos-on-the-jews-natcon-and-couple-of-hindus.html

It is the gospel that shaped the blessings of the West, and not the skin color of those who were so blessed...

The gospel is only for wretches, which the Europe of that day was full of—wretched savages. Being proud of whiteness on that account is like somebody noticing that the first six people who went forward at a Billy Graham crusade all had blue eyes, and concluding from this that blue eyes were the key factor, and not the prayer of repentance...

But all of it was the grace of God, promised centuries before, and not one ounce of it deserved.

"God shall enlarge Japheth, and he shall dwell in the tents of Shem; And Canaan shall be his servant." - Genesis 9:27 (KJV)

And so we see that God is immutable, and the grace of God is immutable. Race? Not so much.

We gladly affirm that all gifts that any man or race possesses come from God, and ought to make their possessors not boastful, but humbly thankful, and deeply impressed with their responsibility to use those gifts for God's glory and the good of man. We are gratified to see Wilson himself later say, "I am very grateful for my ethnic heritage." We join him in this. But—as Wilson admits when describing his American ethnic affections for "football, apple pie...guns, road trips," and so forth—our shared White racial heritage is much more than the gospel and Christianity. We affirm that is the best part, but we deny it is the only part, or the only good part.

Wilson, for example, is wrong to assert that Europe was only full of "wretched savages." The ancient Greeks and Romans were pagan idolaters, but they were not "wretched savages." They were on the whole far more advanced in learning, culture, government, and infrastructure than various remote sub-Saharan African tribes of our own day, not to speak of ancient times. Moving through the centuries, the great medieval church buildings, which Moscow-adjacent classical educators tend to adore, were marvelous, yet they were monuments to superstition more than to true religion. The civilizing power of the Renaissance came at least in part due to the work of esoteric astrologers and self-righteous Romanists. The printing press was not properly a product of the gospel. Neither was the steam engine, or the Internet. Have these things been helps to the progress of the gospel? Absolutely. Are such great inventions in part attributable to how the Christian faith enlightened the European mind, seeing as grace restores and perfects nature? No doubt in part. Can we humbly interpret modern technological advancements as God's gracious and unmerited reward upon Northwestern Europeans for their embrace of the true gospel in the Protestant Reformation? I suppose in part, though the intervening history of Enlightenment unbelief does complicate this question. Moreover, is the present supremacy of the White "Global American Empire" a result of gospel? We love our nation and its greatness, but we would flatter her in her present apostasy if we answered this with an unqualified yes.

In asking these questions, it should be clear to everyone, it is not the gospel alone that has made White men great. To draw on the prophecy Wilson cites approvingly, we do not find that the fulfillment of "God shall enlarge Japheth" is entirely exhausted in the next promise, "And he shall dwell in the tents of Shem." We praise God most of all for supernatural racial blessings, for his leading our Japhetite forefathers to profess faith in Shem's son, the Lord Jesus Christ. But we also distinctly praise him for natural racial blessings, how he has marvelously expanded our fathers above many others on this earth. And in specific, we are grateful for the natural, genetic, and yes, relatively permanent characteristics of our race that, themselves being kind gifts of God, were natural means to the end of this further kind gift of global expansion.

We therefore protest against Wilson, that our distinct gratitude for these distinct blessings by no means shows that we "treat Whiteness as the gospel." That is an unkind false assertion.

Third, we must uncover an unspoken unkindness. Wilson recognized that I referred in passing to one of his articles[68] as one proof that "anti-race realism is the White church party line, which no one may cross with impunity." His present reply further proves this claim. But neither he nor I chose to mention a stronger proof of it, also on his blog, on February 5 of this year. In it he cited a "doxing" thread by a known accuser of the brethren, Blake Callens, written to the harm of particular men associated with a church in Wilson's own ecclesiastical communion. Now, Wilson in that article does tell Callens to "pound sand." Good. But he does so only after naming the church publicly. He alleges, in agreement with Callens' hit piece, that some of the men associated with that church posted various things "offensive to God." Our judgment (echoed here)[69] is that those things were mostly

---

68 https://dougwils.com/books-and-culture/s7-engaging-the-culture/my-360-whiteness-review-comes-in.html

69 https://evangelicaldarkweb.org/2024/02/09/doug-wilsons-third-way-virtue-signal-against-stephen-wolfe-and-crec-church/

just offensive to liberals. That Wilson takes the opportunity to push certain proposed Race and Diversity Memorials[70] does not improve matters, for they are subject to the same criticisms we have brought here. Wilson went on to defend his actions in a February 7 blog post, but we find this defense unconvincing. Moreover, we fear that this present attack against my article merely continues in the same vein of uncharitable dealing with fellow Christians, who are actually more orthodox, and more agreed with him, than his strong assertions make it seem.

Hope

We are sorry to have to write against these absurdities and unkindnesses, but are compelled to do so for the sake of truth and the good name of Christian men. We would conclude however on a more pleasant note, that Pastor Wilson's postscript gave some hope that the conversation may improve.

In it he praises Jeremy Carl's book *The Unprotected Class*, and grants to his readers, tongue in cheek, "You do have permission to start thinking like Jeremy Carl, and so I suggest you hop to it." This book has certain weaknesses in our opinion, but it is important for the cause of race realism in that it documents beyond all doubt the war that's being waged on the White man. And though Wilson will not, or will not yet, grant that race is real, he has granted in this

---

70 https://www.thedailygenevan.com/blog/2023/9/23/on-the-proposed-crec-race-diversity-memorials

postscript that we have a practical need to treat Whiteness as real, because our enemies do so:

*If you lived in a city where the whites and blacks were at daggers drawn, and then one day riots broke out, you don't have to choose up sides. **The other side does that for you.***

It matters not that your mind is full of nuance regarding your Scots/Irish background, which is the only ethnicity (other than American) that you feel any affection for. You need to budget for the fact that other people care very much what color you are, and so it is frankly irrelevant that you don't feel any solidarity with the Dutch, who are the same color as you, and who are hiding in the alley behind the same dumpster that you are.

We ourselves do feel solidarity with the Dutch already, for our shared blood, shared history, shared Protestant religion, and yes, even our shared appearance. But when those who do not are forced at least into the solidarity of shielding themselves from the same anti-White bullets, this is likely to stir up their sympathy for our race realist cause. May the God of Japheth grant this, and deliver our people from all evil.

Appendix III:
Response to Charles Johnson

On July 8, 2024, Charles Johnson replied to the first two chapters of this book (originally published as articles) on race realism. It seemed good to offer a written response here. I thank Mr. Johnson for his engagement on this important issue, and recognize his effort to answer with clarity, order, and logic, and to make Scripture the final rule in all matters of faith and life. I believe all who write on this topic or any other should desire the same.

In sum, I believe Johnson's reply is in some respects uncharitable, and in its arguments does not refute race realism.

Failures in Charity

Johnson labors to be measured throughout, but his reply reveals two failures in charity.

The first is the statement of my ecclesiastical status in his introduction: "Michael Spangler, who was recently deposed from the ministry by the Orthodox Presbyterian Church."

This is not true, and does not charitably protect my name. I was not deposed by judicial process, but divested by administrative process, "without censure, for reasons other than delinquency in faith or life" (OPC Book of Discipline, ch. XXVI, 2). Those who wish to learn more may consider the resources I supplied prior to divestiture in this thread,[71] and this podcast episode.[72]

Johnson's conclusion deepens this misunderstanding: "We would therefore encourage Spangler to repent of this scandalous error, and to heed the admonitions of his church session and of the Orthodox Presbyterian Church, who have sought his repentance from his schismatic and scandalous behavior and positions." Whether my articles themselves contain error or cause schism or scandal is one question. I deny this and will defend them below. But the assertion that my session and the OPC have addressed me is at best vague, and at worst false. Strictly speaking, I have no session. A session is the ruling body of a local church, and since ordination in 2018 I was a member of the regional church and its Presbytery, not a local church. Since divestiture, by the advice of my Presbytery, and in order to keep standing for bringing complaints, I have remained a non-ministerial member of the regional church under the Presbytery of the Southeast of the OPC. More loosely, I can say the Presbytery is my session, but so far they have not spoken to me at all about the articles. If the reference to "scandalous behavior

---

71   https://x.com/spanglermt/status/1778433946029600944
72   Old Paths Podcast: Divested from the Ministry: Interview with Michael Spangler.
     https://open.spotify.com/episode/5MpN78ryTEhKptMq51heWq?
     si=ZjzlJJkLRZWWUyj0osuPLQ&nd=1&dlsi=18d58348d4574717

and positions" was intended to speak of the prior process of divestiture, again, according to the OPC the Book of Discipline, divestiture is not the method used for dealing with scandal.[73]

Second, he from the very first sentence applies the term "racism" to my views. This is uncharitable. Yes the term "racism" in the abstract could possibly describe my position, if only it were taken as a synonym for my preferred term, "race realism." But who takes it this way? Johnson himself recognizes the problem of his choice a few sentences later, when he switches to "racialism" in order to "avoid confusion with simple racial bigotry." In common use "racism" is a highly derogatory term applied to those whom our present ruling powers desire to destroy. To call a man a "racist" in public is to mark him as idiotic and hateful, and to threaten him with permanent unemployment. We of course do not decry the wholesome use of social opprobrium. However, Christians ought to carefully avoid even the appearance of handing fellow Christians over to a worldly outrage mob because of a difference in opinion.

Failures in Argument

As to the substance of his critique, after noting some agreements, Johnson presents sixteen summaries of my arguments each followed by his response, and then adds six

---

73 Nor since the time of writing this reply has any charge been brought, or any other official action that I know of taken by the OPC against my articles. In October 2024 my Presbytery erased me from membership, as I had requested in order to seek membership in another church. I presently (March 2025) am serving as the pastor of a new church plant.

further arguments of his own. I'll address each point, laboring to avoid unnecessary repetition, but taking time to be thorough because of the importance of this issue.

Argument 1.

Acts 17:26–27, God "hath made of one blood all nations of men for to dwell on all the face of the earth, and hath determined the times before appointed, and the bounds of their habitation; that they should seek the Lord."

Johnson's Response. (1) The mere variety of nations does not prove deep racial differences, or racial inferiority. (2) God's will of decree to divide nations should not be confused with a will of precept, that we have a moral duty to maintain those distinctions.

My Answer. (1) Not on its own apart from other arguments, but neither does it disprove them.

(2) Providence is not the moral law, but it has strong weight in determining duty. The fifth commandment, Honor thy father and thy mother, presumes a particular divine providence that has made a certain man my father, and a certain woman my mother. Compare Paul's particular love for a particular people, the Jews, "my brethren, my kinsmen according to the flesh" (Rom. 9:3), which depends on his perception that providence has made the Jews his own people in a way others are not. God has made clear genetic divisions among mankind, of race, nation, tribe, and family. We have a moral duty to recognize those divisions, praise and thank him for them, and observe the greater responsibility we have according to the various relations of proximity they put us in.

This is a standard point in historic Christian teaching. To prove that I supply three testimonies.

Thomas Aquinas (*Summa Theologiae*, II-II, q. 101, art. 1):

> Man is made a debtor to other men in various ways, according to their various excellence and the various benefits he receives from them. In both respects God holds the highest place, since he is most excellent and is for us the first principle of being and government. In the second place, the principles of our being and government are our parents and our fatherland, by whom and in which we have been born and nourished. Therefore, man is a debtor especially to his parents and his fatherland, after God. Hence just as it pertains to religion to worship God, so it pertains to piety, in a secondary degree, to honor one's parents and one's fatherland. Included in the honor given to our parents is the honor given to all our blood relations, since they are called our blood relations because they descend from the same parents, according to the Philosopher. In the honor given to our fatherland is included the honor given to all our fellow-citizens and to all the friends of our fatherland. Therefore piety extends principally to these.[74]

William Ames (*Marrow of Divinity*, bk. 2, ch. 16, "Justice and Charity toward Our Neighbor"):

> 21. But if any apparent disparity appears, either in their nearness to God or to ourselves, then the one who exceeds in any nearness, is more to be beloved—that is, when we cannot exercise the act of our love alike toward all, we are more bound to place our love on those whom God has commended to us by some special nearness or communion,

---

74 Translation cited from here:
https://www.thedailygenevan.com/blog/2022/12/13/naturalcommmunities

than on others. Therefore, even though we should equally will the salvation of others, yet the exercise and care of this will is chiefly due those who are joined near to us in some special respect. For example, though a Soldier ought to wish well to all his fellow Soldiers, yet he is bound to take most care of those who are of the same band, and closest to him in Rank. This appears in that example of Paul, who more fervently desired the conversion of the Israelites than of other Nations. He gives one reason for this affection: because they were his brethren, and kindred according to the flesh, Rom 9.3.

22. Yet in this prerogative of charity, we must wish for those who are near to us, those good things which pertain to that conjunction by which they are near—such as wishing spiritual good things to those who are most spiritually joined to us, and natural good things to those with whom we have a natural nearness. It is not that those kinds of good things are to be separated from one another in our desires, but because of the very kind of conjunction, it is as it were, a beckon from God by which he stirs us up to bestow our pains chiefly in this or that kind.

23. Hence it follows: First, that kindred in blood, *caeteris paribus*, all other things being equal, are more to be beloved than strangers, in those things which pertain to the good things of this life; and among those who are near in blood, those who are nearest are most to be loved.

Petrus van Mastricht (*Theoretical-Practical Theology*, 2.3.2, "Love and Malevolence toward our Neighbor"):

The order of this love is such that, because God is to be cherished with love first and most highly, thus he is the formal reason as it were of love for neighbor. Then closest after God, we love ourselves with that love that aims at true blessedness, for by loving God with a love of union, we immediately love ourselves with the highest love that aims at our spiritual blessedness; and we love others as it were secondarily, as we want them to be partakers with us of the same good. Among men, although no one is to be excluded from our love, yet the same degree of love is not to be observed toward all. Indeed, with regard to the good that we ought to will for our neighbor, there is no inequality, because we ought to will the highest good for each neighbor, as we do for ourselves; nor with regard to the affection of willing or wishing that good ought there be any inequality of intensity and remission. But with regard to the exercise and effects of this affection, an inequality of frequency, order, and extension occurs, as the concurrence of circumstances makes the operation of love necessary. For (1) we ought to elicit more frequently the act itself of charity toward those in whom the reasons and causes of love more frequently come before us. (2) An order ought to be observed according to the occasion that is offered, and the proportion of acts to their objects. (3) There ought to be an extension to more or nobler effects, according to their necessity, and the worthiness of the things loved. See Ames, *Cases of Conscience* (bk. 5, ch. 7, q. 4). Now, with these points introduced generally, among men those are to be loved more than others who draw nearer to God, and in God to ourselves (Gal. 6:10). Consequently, with other things being equal, believers should be loved more than unbelievers; blood relatives, other things being equal, more than strangers; and among blood relatives, those who are more closely conjoined to us than those who are so more distantly, but that according to the nature of the conjunction by which they draw near to us: if the conjunction with someone is physical, physical things are owed more to him; if spiritual, more so spiritual things; that is, if an act of charity that regards both cannot be exercised equally toward both at the same time.

The substance of this response to Argument 1 is repeated various times below, so it seemed worth addressing at greater length.

Argument 2.

Genesis 9, regarding the spreading out of Noah's sons.

Johnson Resp. This again confuses the "indicative and the imperative." And regarding v. 27, "Japheth 'dwelling in Shem's tent' hardly seems like the sort of segregation that Spangler advocates for."

Ans. Again, God's providence in separating mankind into three large racial groupings has moral weight.

Moreover, the prophecy of Japheth's dwelling in the tents of Shem does not oppose all racial segregation. The text itself presumes and does not destroy the distinction between the two racial lines. Nor is geographical proximity, or even some measure domestic cohabitation, itself necessarily race-mixing. The mere presence of a minority of foreign strangers in a household or nation—e.g. Abraham and his foreign servant Eliezer of Damascus (Gen. 15:2), or Israel and its foreign residents like Ebed-melech the Ethiopian (Jer. 38:7)—in itself brings no dilution of their racial identity. In fact, common experience among today's American Southerners teaches that geographical proximity to other races can in fact increase one's reasonable conviction of the imprudence of mixing with them.

However, we believe v. 27 is most properly taken as a figure for the conversion of the Japhetites, dwelling in the tents of Shem by believing in Shem's son Jesus Christ. This is notably fulfilled in the New Testament progress of the gospel throughout the Roman empire, then to Northern Europe and its colonies. This advance of the true religion in no way taught the propriety of racial mixing. In fact, when Protestant Japhetites in their colonizing efforts found themselves in close proximity to highly distinct racial groups, they notably enacted laws against miscegenation, as we proved from American history. And just as notably, the Papists, whom Johnson and I agree are grossly corrupted in religion, followed a policy of racial mixing which resulted in the large mestizo populations that today inhabit the nations they colonized.

Argument 3.

Gen. 10:32, "after their generations."

Johnson Resp. This is irrelevant.

Ans. It is not irrelevant: it is a clear scriptural statement that races are differentiated from each other, and into their various subordinate nations, in the normal course of natural generation. Race and ethnicity are genetic realities.

Argument 4.

"The Bible says people are different colors and passes some aesthetic judgment on it, in Jer. 13.23, Acts 8:27, Song. 1:5-6, Gen. 10:6, Lam. 4:7-8, 1 Sam. 16:12, Song 5:10, etc."

Johnson Resp. (1) In Song 1:5, "black" and "comely" are not opposed. (2) Metaphors of light and dark to speak of moral things do not presume aesthetic judgments. (3) The Bible "places very little value on physical beauty," per Prov. 31:30 and 1 Peter 3:3–4.

Ans. (1) "Black" and "comely" are opposites. This is a standard historic interpretation of this verse, and fits well with v. 6, "Look not upon me, because I am black, because the sun hath looked upon me." On this address to the "daughters of Jerusalem," James Durham explains,[75]

> First then (saith she) I answer, by conceding what is truth, I am black, both with crosses and corruptions, that cannot be denied. 2. She qualifies her concession, though I be black, yet I am comely, that is, I am not universally or altogether unlovely, mine estate is mixed, being made up of crosses and comforts, corruptions and graces, beauty and blacknesse.

(2) Metaphors of light and dark do presume aesthetic judgments. White is universally recognized as a color of purity, and is accordingly opposed to black. Of course the color black, or dark brown, considered in itself has its own proper beauty, as do Black people, but all we asserted was that Scripture "passes some aesthetic judgment." This assertion stands.

(3) The Bible often speaks of relative importance in absolute terms. Prov. 31:30, "Beauty is vain," needs to be read in light of God's own commendation of physical beauty (Gen. 12:11; 26:7; 29:17; etc.), even in terms of fair skin (in David, 1 Sam. 16:12;and metaphorically in Christ, Song 5:10).

---

75 https://quod.lib.umich.edu/e/eebo/A37032.0001.001/1:4.2.5?
    rgn=div3;view=fulltext

Argument 5.

Geographical separation of the nations.

Johnson Resp. "Again, a great difference lies between the indicative and the imperative." Travel is sometimes required, Gen. 12:1, etc., and movement of peoples or individuals not forbidden.

Ans. Travel and movement in themselves do not themselves imply any racial mixing, or deny that races have their own proper geographical homes. The millions of immigrants crossing the U.S. border, documented or not, are no less foreign for setting their feet on American soil. Modern migration has pressed ethnic boundaries, but not destroyed them: China is still overwhelmingly ethnically Chinese, India still Indian, etc. Many migrants still consider their foreign land their proper home. Africans who have been in the United States for centuries still call themselves "African-Americans." Similarly, the Hebrew slaves in Egypt were still called Hebrews even at their emancipation four hundred years after migrating there.

Argument 6.

"People speak different languages."

Johnson Resp. (1) "Many languages are spoken by multiple races, and no race speaks just one language," e.g. Paul, whose multilingual cross-cultural ministry was not "an abomination." (2) At best this argues cultural, not racial difference. (3) Blacks and Whites both speak English, does this not mean they have closer kinship than Whites of different nations?

Ans. (1) Any capable person can learn foreign languages, but the languages are still foreign. The universal phenomenon of distinct "native tongues" is a strong witness to racial and ethnic divisions. To imply a Christian race realist would call foreign language preaching an "abomination" is gratuitous. We assert instead that it is a necessary part of the fulfillment of the church's great commission (Matt. 28:19).

(2) Culture and race are distinct, but usually not separable. We grant language in the abstract is separable from genetics. However, it does not follow from this that culture broadly conceived has no genetic basis.

(3) White and Blacks in the U.S. do have a linguistic affinity. But there are other significant respects in which Whites in far-removed nations have more affinity with each other than with Blacks in their own lands. And the well-known differences between White and Black English are clear enough linguistic markers of their racial division.

Argument 7.

"National sins exist. The Canaanites were exterminated."

Johnson Resp. (1) General national sins have exceptions in individuals. They are imputed to individuals only insofar as they are individually guilty of them. National sins change over time and place. (2) This would imply "that kinship between honest, godly, protestant Blacks and Whites is far greater than the kinship between Christian Whites and heathen, atheist, or Roman Catholic Whites."

Ans. (1) Of course there are individual exceptions. But when speaking of groups, we have to speak generally, in terms of aggregates and averages. If we cannot do this, we cannot say anything meaningful of any race or nation as a whole. We grant plainly with Peter, "Of a truth I perceive that God is no respecter of persons: but in every nation he that feareth him, and worketh righteousness, is accepted with him" (Acts 10:34). This is not the point in question.

(2) We gladly affirm spiritual affinity between sincere Protestant Blacks and Whites. And moreover, that this is the best and most precious form of affinity: "To the saints that are in the earth, and to the excellent, in whom is all my delight" (Ps. 16:3). But spiritual affinity does not remove many other weighty marks of difference between races, nor their importance.

Argument 8.

"Some nations rule over others. Canaan shall be a 'servant of servants.' "'Servant of servants" would aptly describe the future fate of many of Ham's black African children.'"

Johnson Resp. (1) Rule comes from God's sovereign choice, not immutable or inherent superiority. God gave Israel greatness not for any merit in them, Deut. 7:6–7. And he removes superiority from nations for proudly attributing it to their own virtue. (2) "There is no biblical basis upon which to assert that sub-Saharan Africans are descendants of Ham."

Ans. (1) Yes, "God is the judge: he putteth down one, and setteth up another" (Ps. 75:7). But to assert he never does this, at least in part, by granting in providence certain intrinsic racial characteristics fitting to rule, or to subjection, goes too far. We may speak of mercy or grace in God's giving of natural gifts, in order to cultivate thankfulness, and destroy all pride and arrogance, which God hates. But temporal rule is usually in part a matter of natural endowments, and we do not usually speak of strictly natural abilities as gifts of mercy, at least not of saving mercy, but rather as gifts of God's more general kindness and love for man. Moreover, if a gift is truly natural to a man, it is immutable in the respect that if it changed, it would require a change in his nature. God can make such a change, but he does not commonly do so. There is an analogy with races and nations: though they are subject to some change, usually in the long term, the natural characteristics that distinguish them are fairly permanent and stable, at least over the course of a normal human lifetime.

Compare Samuel Rutherford (*Lex Rex*, q. 13):

> "The degree or order of subjection natural is a subjection in respect of gifts or age: so Aristotle (*Politics* 1.3) says, "Some are by nature servants." His meaning is good, that some gifts of nature, such as natural wisdom or aptitude to govern, have made some men of gold, fitter to command, and some of iron and clay, fitter to be servants and slaves...
>
> Aquinas (II-II. q. 57. art. 3). Driedo (*De libert. Christ.* bk.1, p. 8). following Aristotle, (*Politics* 7.14) hold, though man had never sinned, there should have been a sort of dominion of the more gifted and wiser above the less wise and weaker, not antecedent from nature, properly, but consequent, for the utility and good of the weaker, insofar as it is good for the weaker to be guided by the stronger, which cannot be denied to have some ground in nature."

We address a practical point Johnson raises here. He asks, "Will God not also judge the European or the White American who boasts that his power and prosperity is a result of his own merit and not God's mercy?" We answer, yes, and duly warned. But we ask in return, "Will not God judge the European or the White American who in false humility refuses to take up the responsibility of his God-given superiority in order to serve others, and promote Christ's kingdom?"

(2) We leave the informed reader to Johnson's argument from linguistics. It seems fairly evident to us that sub-Saharan Africans are descendants of Ham, if only because Jer. 13:23, "Can the Ethiopian change his skin?" attributes notably distinct skin to the "Cushite" (per the literal Hebrew), and Cush was a son of Ham (Gen. 10:6), as Johnson admits. Samuel Bochart, a French Protestant, was considered an expert on these matters in the 17th century: in his *Geographia Sacra*[76] he asserts that in the division of the world, Ham received, among other places, "Egypt and all Africa." He goes on to affirm a common speculation, which we echoed in our second article:

> In Hebrew *cham* means hot, and *chum* black. Thus the name of Ham came either from heat or from blackness. Nor does this seem to have happened apart from the divine will, since the Africa that fell to Ham labors under immoderate heat, and nearly all his posterity were burned and darkened by the intensity of the nearby star.

---

76 https://www.digitale-sammlungen.de/en/view/bsb10326496?page=174

Argument 9.

"Nations have different religions."

Johnson Resp. (1) Spangler uses testimonies only from the Old Testament. "How foolish," given the promise that Egyptians will know the Lord, etc. (Isa. 19:21–25). (2) This implies a strong kinship between Protestant Christians of any race.

Ans. (1) I note he answers with a testimony from the Old Testament. I affirm Ps. 72:11, "All nations shall serve him," and that remarkable progress has been made toward this already under the New Testament. No doubt Johnson would affirm with me that for a pagan nation to put away its false gods is a miraculous work of God's grace (Jer. 2:11), as it was among our White pagan ancestors. But we should not make generalizations about race according to miracles, and certainly not unknown future miracles. For example, I reasonably expect "Indians are Hindus" to be a safe generalization at least for the rest of my lifetime, though I pray and long for the day when India will bow the knee to Jesus Christ.

(2) We answered this above under Argument 7, (2).

Argument 10.

"Israel's civil law implies a certain level of nationalism."

Johnson Resp. (1) If so, to exceed that level is sin by excess. Forbidding interracial marriages is a sin by excess. (2) Nationalism does not mean "racism." "Black Americans and

White Americans all pertain to the same state and nation, and are 'natural born citizens.'"

Ans. (1) This is not how the general equity of the Old Testament civil law is applied. If we agree nationalism is a principle of general equity, then the manner of its civil application depends on prudent observation of our contemporary circumstances. As the civil law of Israel has expired, nations today are not bound to its particular limits and degrees, only to its equity. However, we are bound to recognize that none of the particular laws of Israel, being divinely given, were unjust in themselves. Given therefore that at least certain interracial marriages were forbidden in Israel's civil law, Deut. 7:3, it cannot be true that legal prohibition of certain interracial marriages is a sin in the abstract. It would have to be proven to be sin in the concrete circumstances.

(2) We note the recurring term "racism." We also note the failure to divide the question, and the begging of the question, that Blacks and Whites "pertain to the same state and nation." It is evident that Blacks pertain to the same state as Whites in the U.S., having been given legal citizenship. That they are of the same nation presumes membership in a nation can be entirely separated from blood ancestry, which we deny. They are a distinct Black nation, "African-Americans."

Argument 11.

Israel's tribal land ownership.

Johnson Resp. "The specific laws concerning the inalienability of property in Canaan were typological," citing Matthew Henry on the Jubilee, and on the distinction on this point with the laws of England.

Ans. Yes, the civil law taught spiritual truths, and pictured future spiritual realities. This did not make it no longer a true civil law, or remove its general equity. Israel and Judah's kings were certainly types of Christ. Yet this did not mean Samuel Rutherford was wrong to draw many political lessons from those kings in his book Lex Rex. So for all other sound use of the Bible in political theory, or in various branches of philosophy and science. Nor was England required to replicate the Mosaic civil law in its details, only in its equity.

Argument 12.

"Israelite law discriminated against foreigners in matters of slavery and interest."

Johnson Resp. Political difference does not imply "profound intellectual, moral, and religious differences between different races."

Ans. Lawful discrimination between ethnic Israelites and foreigners in the civil law shows more than a "political difference." It is a witness to the reality of ethnic difference, which precedes and is presumed by the legal distinctions in question. "Israelite" and "sojourner" are not categories created by the law, but rather observed by it. Ethnic difference is not merely political. We grant this smaller argument in itself it does not bear the weight of our whole case: it is one small witness among many to the reality of racial difference.

Argument 13.

"Israelite law required that their ruler be a fellow Jew."

Johnson Resp. "Our commonwealth has a similar law in the constitution that the president be a 'natural born citizen.' But a law requiring he be White would be of quite a different nature. Like the last point, this one confuses citizenship and race."

Ans. It is rather Johnson's response that confuses citizenship and race. We grant that removing racial rules for citizenship in America has contributed to this confusion. But in light of the history of early America, in which all "natural born citizens" were White, the requirement of a native president was a racial requirement, just as it was in Deuteronomy 17:15.

Argument 14.

"Israelite law required separation from foreigners."

Johnson Resp. This was for the sake of religion. "Converts to Judaism, however, were integrated into the people and their offspring were afforded all civil rights and privileges of full-blooded Israelites." The assimilation of Ruth testifies against the "one-drop rule" of American segregation.

Ans. It remains to be proven that there were no other reasons for the laws in question than religion. Did God not at all desire to preserve his people's ethnic identity for its own sake, out of love for them? Should not we? Or might not there be other other evils and inconveniences besides false religion that those laws were intended to prevent? Or that such laws wisely applied today could also prevent?

Even if they were only for religion, this would lend a strong argument to the equity of such requirements today, e.g. strictly forbidding all Hindu immigration to the United States. However, note that the laws in question are written in ethnic terms, naming particular nations (e.g. Deut. 7), though with religious reasons given (v. 4). So properly the analogy would be a law today forbidding Indian immigration to America, for the sake of preventing the influence of Hinduism. Would Mr. Johnson affirm such a law?

Moreover, it is simply false to assert that converts to Judaism, simply because they were converted, "were integrated into the people and their offspring were afforded all civil rights and privileges of full-blooded Israelites." Johnson cites Num. 9:14, which only says that strangers may keep the Passover. His claim confuses the two kingdoms of Christ, the church and the state, the spiritual and the temporal, which two things were clearly distinct in both Old and New Testament. It is analogous to saying that when a foreign visitor is converted in an American church, he and his children thereby become American.

Such a claim might be expected from an Erastian, or a Voluntaryist, but not from a Presbyterian Establishmentarian. George Gillespie rejects it in his refutation of Erastianism in

Aaron's Rod Blossoming,[77] saying of Old Testament proselytes (citing with approval John Selden, though himself an Erastian),

> They were initiated into the Jewish religion by circumcision, baptism, and sacrifice; and they were allowed not only to worship God apart by themselves, but also to come into the church and congregation of Israel, and to be called by the name of Jews,—nevertheless, they were restrained and excluded from dignities, magistracies and preferments in the Jewish republic, and from divers marriages which were free to the Israelites, even as strangers initiated and associated into the church of Rome have not therefore the privilege of Roman citizens. Thus Mr. Selden, who hath thereby made it manifest that there was a distinction of the Jewish church and Jewish state, because those proselytes, being embodied into the Jewish church as church members, and having a right to communicate in the holy ordinances among the rest of the people of God, yet were not properly members of the Jewish state, nor admitted to civil privileges; whence it is also that the names of Jews and proselytes were used distinctly, Acts ii. 10.

Also, we did and do affirm that marriage is a means of ethnic assimilation, citing the case of Ruth and Boaz. This of course is presumed by every historic law against inter-racial marriage: the whole purpose of them was to prevent undue or harmful ethnic assimilation. Moreover, the "one-drop rule" was not universal in historic American jurisprudence, and it should not be used to mock the difficulty of determining exact ethnic boundaries when answering relevant legal questions. Hard cases do not make laws impossible.

---

77 https://archive.org/details/aaronsrodblossom00gill/page/4/mode/1up

Argument 15.

"The burden of proof lies on those who would prove that interracial marriages are lawful."

Johnson Resp. "On the contrary, the doctrine of Christian liberty and liberty of conscience demands that the burden of proof always lie on the one who would prove something unlawful. See Dt. 12:32, as well as chapter 20 of the Westminster Confession."

Ans. Mr. Johnson fairly accurately summarized my arguments above, but here he has not. This is what I said on this point in chapter 2, emphasis added:

In light of all these things, if some would assert that race realism in general, or in specific a preference for intra-ethnic or intra-racial marriage, is unique to the Old Testament economy, and not at all a matter of universal, permanent, general equity, we would simply say here, the burden of proof for this assertion rests entirely on them.

This was barely an assertion on my part. I softened it rhetorically on purpose to gain a better hearing for a view that I know many find very offensive, and which I promised to expand upon later. To speak more directly here, I do not assert that inter-ethnic or inter-racial marriage is in itself unlawful, strictly forbidden in all its forms by Scripture and nature, as in the case of so-called "gay marriage." I did and do affirm there are examples of it in Scripture, and though examples do not themselves make law, I do not assert that they are all bad examples. What I do assert is this, that given various serious factors—the enormous importance of the choice of one's spouse, the weighty consequences that choice brings for the couple, their children, their family, and their nation, the blessings that come from affinity and similarity in marriage, the special love we owe to family, kin, and nation, the differences God has established in providence between races and nations, the woeful reality of racial strife, which appears only to be increasing, and other not insignificant special challenges that come to spouses and their children through inter-racial marriage—it is usually not wise, not prudent, not best to marry across a large ethnic boundary, and all the less so the greater that boundary is. And yes, we do affirm, as should all people, that it is a sin not to be wise, not to be prudent, and not to choose the best we can, even among things that may be lawful in themselves.

To address Mr. Johnson's concern directly: I do not assert that what is unlawful is inter-racial marriage *per se*. Rather, what is unlawful is to be imprudent. And inter-racial marriage is often imprudent. Indeed in some extreme forms it is always imprudent, or at least so often imprudent that rules should be enforced against it, in the family, or even in the state, as in Christian America until 1967.

I believe this has fully answered the charge from Deut. 12:32, against adding to God's Word, or as it more popularly expressed, "That's legalism!" It is not legalism. It is wisdom, and we ignore it at our peril.

Argument 16.

"'A special love for kin and nation is a part of natural affection.'"

Johnson Resp. "Am I, a White man from Wisconsin, closer kin to a White Russian speaker in Siberia than a Black man that lives next door?" Christ in Luke 10 says the Samaritan was more a neighbor to the injured man than were the priest and Levite.

Ans. Yes, you are closer racial kin to the White man, though you are have more affinity with the Black neighbor in other ways. In Luke 10 Christ commends an example of mercy toward a nearby stranger in immediate need, and condemns the self-righteous withholding of love from him. We affirm this heartily, and deny that special love for kin and nation oppose this in the least. Luke 10:36–37 and 1 Timothy 5:8 are in perfect harmony.

Johnson's Arguments

We move now to Johnson's own arguments against racialism, with my answers.

1. **"Children from unlawful unions are cursed in Scripture. But children from interracial marriages are not cursed. Therefore, they are not unlawful."**

Ans. This is answered well enough in Argument 15 above. We do not affirm the parallel of fornication and interracial marriage. Also, either his major premise is false, or his logic unsound. For the syllogism to work the major premise would have to be, "All children from all unlawful unions are cursed in Scripture," but his citations of Scripture only prove this is so for some children from some unlawful unions.

For his refutation of the potential objection from the Ammonites and Moabites, we refer the reader to Argument 14 above.

2. "No prohibition exists on these marriages. Therefore, they are not prohibited."

Ans. See Argument 15 above.

3. The lowest-level biological category in Scripture, across the boundaries of which miscegenation is forbidden, is the species-level boundary. Therefore, it is not racial boundaries."

Ans. We affirm mixing of man with other species is unlawful and perverted, Lev. 18:23. "It is confusion." As explained in Argument 15 above, we do not ascribe the same manner of unlawfulness to inter-racial marriage. Yet there is a principle of equity in this law, against undue confusion of things God has made separate. That principle remains relevant to the question of inter-racial marriage.

4. "The universal moral laws of Scripture, such as the ten commandments and the law of love, do not command segregation or sanction racism, but rather, they are inconsistent with it."

Ans. This is a mere assertion, not proven, as if there were no possible respect in which morality or love could inform a moderate separation of races according to prudence.

The rhetorical question that follows is gratuitous:

Can it be imagined that such scenes that we have witnessed under Jim Crow in the United States such as refusing to serve food to paying black customers, allocating inferior facilities to them, denying them the use of the courts and the protection of the laws, refusing to admit them to schools and universities, and the use of racial violence to maintain white supremacy are consistent with laws like "love your neighbor as yourself"?

The various assertions of sin here are not permissible without clear proof and defining of terms. If they are false, they are slanders of an entire people, indeed the author's own ethnic and political countrymen, most of them professors of his own Christian religion. The assumption that they can be asserted without proof, as common knowledge, we fear reveals an unthinking submission to a false historical narrative. They also are strange exceptions to the measured academic tone observed elsewhere in Johnson's reply.

He then suggests a possible objection, "Black and white people are not neighbors." This is grasping at straws. No sane White Christian would deny various respects in which Blacks in his own country are his neighbors, and much less deny that he should show them mercy when they are in need, as he has opportunity. Race realists by no means deny the duty of love of neighbor, of all men, even of enemies. Rather, they affirm that true love is ordered, acting more strongly according as bonds of affinity are stronger, as explained above by Aquinas, Ames, and Mastricht, and that one important bond of affinity, among others, is race.

5. "All of mankind is alike created and renewed in the image of God in 'knowledge, righteousness and holiness.' Therefore, there are not the profound intellectual, moral, and spiritual differences Spangler posits."

Ans. If he speaks only of truly converted Christians, this has little relevance for discussing racial or political matters, as most men are not renewed in the image of God. But even only among Christians, his arguments are not sound. Conversion does not change a man's natural intelligence. Conversion does remove the dominion of sin, but not its presence, nor a man's natural proclivities toward certain sins. No doubt truly converted American Indians generally have to struggle harder against abusing alcohol. Conversion does not immediately remove all religious differences either: the religion of Christian Blacks in America is notably different from that of Christian Whites, even among the best examples of the most sincere and godly people, and even within churches that claim the same ecclesiastical tradition.

6. "When Miriam and Aaron complain against Moses on the basis of his mixed race marriage, God sides with Moses. Therefore, their complaint was baseless."

Ans. This argument fails to make proper distinctions. The main complaint was against Moses' authority, Num. 12:2, "Hath the LORD indeed spoken only by Moses?" It appears the claim against his Ethiopian wife was secondary to this, as God's response in vv. 6–8 does not address it. Therefore, if Miriam and Aaron are alleging against Moses the charge of impropriety in marrying a foreigner, it does not follow that because they were punished for opposing Moses' authority by this, that there is therefore never impropriety in marrying foreigners.

We also should be careful not to allege a greater degree of racial mixing that was actually involved in this marriage. It seems to us the wife in question was Zipporah the Midianite, called an "Ethiopian" (lit. "Cushite") because the Midianites lived in the region sometimes called Cush. If this is so, Midian was a son of Abraham by Keturah (Gen. 25:2), so racially speaking, not very distant from Moses.

Conclusion

Again, I affirm Mr. Johnson has made an effort to address this difficult matter with clarity, order, logic, and submission to the Scriptures. This is much preferable to the unthinking denunciations that often pass for discourse about race, even among Christians. I for one welcome many more such efforts. But as noted above this particular reply has failed to convict the present author of "scandalous behavior and positions." I leave readers to consider the rest of my series on race realism.

For further reading, I also highly recommend the essay "Natural Communities"[78] by Michael Hunter, which, though published in 2022, is quite useful for addressing Mr. Johnson's arguments.

---

78 https://www.thedailygenevan.com/blog/2022/12/13/naturalcommmunities

Appendix IV:
Response to David Vogel

David Vogel, a minister in the Orthodox Presbyterian Church, published a response[79] on October 24, 2024 to this book (at that time published as online articles). In reply, I'll not repeat what I have said in my chapter answering objections, or my replies to Charles Johnson and Douglas Wilson. Instead I will briefly address a few particular features of this response.

First, at the beginning Rev. Vogel expresses a misgiving about writing at all: "I don't want to elevate fringe voices by engaging with them." But why are race realists on the fringe? This was not so mere decades ago. The greatest men of the American Presbyterian church were race realists, even segregationists, as I showed in chapter 4.

Moreover, the implied argument against "fringe voices" is not strong. Let me take the liberty to restate it more explicitly: "Michael Spangler's views have since the 1960s been increasingly marked as low-status and unintelligent, and those who hold them banished from polite society. And no Christian wants to be banished from polite society, right?" A

---

79 https://davidvogel.net/2024/10/24/against-spanglers-race-realism/

tacit appeal is being made to the consensus of the most degenerate era of our nation's history. This is not good.

Second, in the midst of the discussion of racial differences, he makes an interjection:

> (At this point, I should pause to note my own discomfort at interacting with these ideas. It is not pleasant to have to entertain the hypothesis—even for the purpose of rebuttal —that my black friends and neighbors are seriously morally and intellectually deficient. I am sure it is even less pleasant for them to be the subject of such speculation. Sadly, ugly ideas can only be rebutted with ugly debates.)

In expressing his emotional and aesthetic distaste, Rev. Vogel clearly tells his audience that he finds our views disgusting. Yet without clear reasons clearly argued for such disgust, this is only a "virtue signal," that he is not part of the unwashed mass of racist Christians. This is not impressive to a serious and thoughtful reader. Refusing out of mere distaste even to entertain that "friends and neighbors" could in fact in some respect be racial inferiors, is no less wrong because the refusal cloaks itself in tender sensitivity.

Third, regarding racial differences in morality, Rev. Vogel suggests that because of "socioeconomic factors" that also affect poor white communities, the obvious criminality of Blacks cannot support a generalization about any moral defect of their race. But this makes no sense. It doesn't matter if Black crime is occasioned by Black poverty. The generalization remains sound. "Blacks are violent" is a true statement, whatever the causes. However, if Rev. Vogel had bothered to read the article I'd cited,[80] he'd have seen the author argued his claim while painstakingly controlling for socioeconomic factors. A salient quote:

> All else being equal in terms of household income during adolescence, black men are four times as likely to find themselves behind bars as white men.
>
> That's a huge disparity. For instance, black men at the 98th percentile of upbringing, the best-behaved black cohort, are jailed as often as white men at the 50th percentile. Similarly, the black rate at the national median of income is 7.2 percent, a little higher than the white rate at the single lowest percentile.
>
> That suggests that there is approximately a two standard deviation difference in racial propensity to be prison-bound, even when controlling for affluence when young.

Within this discussion Rev. Vogel makes a parenthetical assertion that many of the alleged socioeconomic factors "are rooted in generational sins against black Americans by their white neighbors." But for this strong assertion against his own race, he offers no proof at all.

Fourth, regarding racial differences in intelligence, Rev. Vogel casts up a cloud of suspicion by making suggestions, without argument, about "biased tests" and "racist motivations," though these objections are patiently answered in the works I cited. He then cites a study about increases in IQ in some nations in the decades after WWII, concluding, "It is absurd to hastily draw causal conclusions about the observed gap between black and white IQ test results." But

---

80 Steve Sailer, "America's Black Male Problem," *Taki's Magazine*, February 15, 2023. (https://www.takimag.com/article/americas-black-male-problem/)

nothing Rev. Vogel said at all disproves the assertion in question, that Blacks are significantly less intelligent than Whites.

Fifth, regarding inferiority and superiority, Rev. Vogel quotes the Westminster Larger Catechism Q. 124, that "superiors" include those who are superior in "gifts." But then in the next paragraph he says, "Authority in Scripture is consistently a matter of position, not natural endowment." So is Rev. Vogel implying that the Catechism exceeds Scripture? Or did he forget what he just quoted? Or does he think superiority in gifts does not in any respect grant authority among those who are otherwise equal?

Sixth and finally, I would mention Rev. Vogel's inclusion of two screenshots of X posts that I reposted:

Michael Spangler reposted

Andy Taylor @soandytaylor · 5h
Despite @douglaswils warnings I'm going
to race realism even harder now.

⬭ 10   ⇄ 9   ♡ 61   ılıl 2.6K   🔖 ⅋

The second was prefaced with, "I do not know what sort of prideful folly can make the sentiment expressed below seem fitting for a Christian."

I am frankly at a loss to know what's wrong with these two posts. It is not sinful to have fun while celebrating our own race. And if the mere appearance of a white man set in contrast with men of other races (to my mind, portrayed honorably and fairly) is a tacit argument for white supremacy, then so be it. It is not a matter for white shame that white racial nobility can be noted at a glance. Nor is it proud to recognize this blessing with thankfulness to God who gave it.

I leave to interested readers to consider Rev. Vogel's response further, and to compare it with what I have written elsewhere.

I conclude by noting with thankfulness the concessions he makes to my arguments. He begins his response with an affirmation that race is indeed real: "The fact that there are recognizable races is obvious and uncontroversial." And he concludes admitting in his own way the great racial problems in our nation:

> I am troubled by the explicit anti-whiteness espoused by some parts of the political left…. I also believe our present almost uncontrolled flow of illegal immigration is dangerous to our nation, and that limits on immigration are not at all contrary to Christian charity.

This is good, and I am grateful for such agreement. Yet these matters are not so obvious to all. The reality of race is explicitly and publicly denied by prominent ministers in Rev. Vogel's own church, like Dr. David Van Drunen. And such a denial is at the root of the evils he sees done against the White man in our day. If Rev. Vogel cannot fully agree with our conclusions, we would at the least welcome him to continue writing in defense of our shared affirmation:

Race is real.

Other books currently available from Sacra Press:

A Treatise of Christian Religion
by Thomas Cartwright
Father of the Puritans & of Presbyterianism displays the full jewels of a systematic theology in a catechetical format. Newly republished for the first time in centuries.

The Old Faith
by Henry Bullinger
Titanic Swiss Reformer weaves a mixed work of biblical & covenant theology, born of pastoral concerns, to prove the antiquity of the Christian Faith.

Lectures On Human Nature
by Samuel Doak
18th century American Presbyterian, church-planter, and school teacher keenly pens an introductory philosophy of human nature. Includes his sermon to the Overmountain Men just before their victory at King's Mountain.

A Precept for the Baptism of Infants
by Nathaniel Stephens
17th century non-conformist Minister proves the precept of paedobaptism from the New Testament in response to the objection of anti-paedobaptists.

The Cambridge & Saybrook Platforms
by Miscellaneous Ministers
New England Congregationalists inscribe their polity.

Books soon-to-be or now published by Sacra Press:

On the First Sin of Adam
by Franciscus Junius
French Protestant Reformer and theologian explores Adam's first sin and its relation to God's foreknowledge and decree, necessity, and free will.

The System of Political Discipline
by Bartholomew Keckermann
Late 16th century German Reformed scholar, philosopher, and theologian masterfully and methodically constructs an impressive, systematic work of political theory.

The Christian Obligations of Citizenship
by John G. Sheppard
19th century Anglican academic exploits logic, rhetoric, history, classical sources, and Scripture to construct his Christian political theory.

Positive Christianity in the Third Reich
by Cajus Fabricius
Protestant Theologian and NSDAP party member writes to show the compatibility between National Socialism and a certain form of Christianity. Includes The 28 Theses of the German Christians & miscellaneous documents (newly translated) of Fabricius.

With many more to come—Lord willing.

Visit www.sacrapress.com/armory to purchase available books, to stay updated on releases, and more.